Contents

		Page
Introduction		iv

Question and answer bank

Chapter tasks		Questions	Answers
Chapter 1	Costing techniques	3	137
Chapter 2	Statistical techniques	16	155
Chapter 3	Standard costing	29	167
Chapter 4	Variance analysis	32	170
Chapter 5	Operating statements	46	191
Chapter 6	Interpreting variances	59	205
Chapter 7	Performance indicators	75	226
Chapter 8	Cost management	113	259
Chapter 9	Activity based costing (ABC)	117	262
Chapter 10	Decision making techniques	122	267
AAT AQ2016 sample assessment 1		281	297
AAT AQ2016 sample assessment 2		309	
BPP practice assessment 1		311	325
BPP practice assessment 2		337	353
BPP practice assessment 3		367	381

Introduction

This is BPP Learning Media's AAT Question Bank for *Management Accounting: Decision and Control*. It is part of a suite of ground-breaking resources produced by BPP Learning Media for AAT assessments.

This Question Bank has been written in conjunction with the BPP Course Book, and has been carefully designed to enable students to practise all of the learning outcomes and assessment criteria for the units that make up *Management Accounting: Decision and Control*. It is fully up to date as at April 2018 and reflects both the AAT's qualification specification and the sample assessments provided by the AAT.

This Question Bank contains these key features:

- Tasks corresponding to each chapter of the Course Book. Some tasks are designed for learning purposes, others are of assessment standard

- AAT's AQ2016 sample assessment 1 and answers for *Management Accounting: Decision and Control* and further BPP practice assessments

The emphasis in all tasks and assessments is on the practical application of the skills acquired.

VAT

You may find tasks throughout this Question Bank that need you to calculate or be aware of a rate of VAT. This is stated at 20% in these examples and questions.

Approaching the assessment

When you sit the assessment it is very important that you follow the on screen instructions. This means you need to carefully read the instructions, both on the introduction screens and during specific tasks.

When you access the assessment you should be presented with an introductory screen with information similar to that shown below (taken from the introductory screen from one of the AAT's AQ2016 sample assessments for *Management Accounting: Decision and Control*).

We have provided this **practice assessment** to help you familiarise yourself with our e-assessment environment. It is designed to demonstrate as many as possible of the question types that you may find in a live assessment. It is not designed to be used on its own to determine whether you are ready for a live assessment.

At the end of this practice assessment you will receive an immediate assessment result. This will only take into account your responses to tasks 1 - 4 and 6 as these are the elements of the assessment that are computer marked. In the live assessment, your responses to tasks 5, 7 and 8 will be human marked.

Assessment information:

You have **2 hours and 30 minutes** to complete this practice assessment.

This assessment contains **8 tasks** and you should attempt to complete **every** task.
Each task is independent. You will not need to refer to your answers to previous tasks.
Read every task carefully to make sure you understand what is required.

Tasks 5, 7 and 8 require extended writing as part of your response to the questions. You should make sure you allow adequate time to complete these tasks.

Where the date is relevant, it is given in the task data.
Both minus signs and brackets can be used to indicate negative numbers **unless** task instructions say otherwise.

You must use a full stop to indicate a decimal point. For example, write 100.57 NOT 100,57 or 100 57
You may use a comma to indicate a number in the thousands, but you don't have to. For example, 10000 and 10,000 are both acceptable.

The actual instructions will vary depending on the subject you are studying for. It is very important you read the instructions on the introductory screen and apply them in the assessment. You don't want to lose marks when you know the correct answer just because you have not entered it in the right format.

In general, the rules set out in the AAT sample assessments for the subject you are studying for will apply in the real assessment, but you should carefully read the information on this screen again in the real assessment, just to make sure. This screen may also confirm the VAT rate used if applicable.

A full stop is needed to indicate a decimal point. We would recommend using minus signs to indicate negative numbers and leaving out the comma signs to indicate thousands, as this results in a lower number of key strokes and less margin for error when working under time pressure. Having said that, you can use whatever is easiest for you as long as you operate within the rules set out for your particular assessment.

You have to show competence throughout the assessment and you should therefore complete all of the tasks. Don't leave questions unanswered.

In some assessments, written or complex tasks may be human marked. In this case you are given a blank space or table to enter your answer into. You are told in the assessments which tasks these are (note: there may be none if all answers are marked by the computer).

If these involve calculations, it is a good idea to decide in advance how you are going to lay out your answers to such tasks by practising answering them on a word document, and certainly you should try all such tasks in this Question Bank and in the AAT's environment using the sample assessment.

When asked to fill in tables, or gaps, never leave any blank even if you are unsure of the answer. Fill in your best estimate.

Note that for some assessments where there is a lot of scenario information or tables of data provided (eg tax tables), you may need to access these via 'pop-ups'. Instructions will be provided on how you can bring up the necessary data during the assessment.

Finally, take note of any task specific instructions once you are in the assessment. For example you may be asked to enter a date in a certain format or to enter a number to a certain number of decimal places.

Grading

To achieve the qualification and to be awarded a grade, you must pass all the mandatory unit assessments, all optional unit assessments (where applicable) and the synoptic assessment.

The AAT Level 4 Professional Diploma in Accounting will be awarded a grade. This grade will be based on performance across the qualification. Unit assessments and synoptic assessments are not individually graded. These assessments are given a mark that is used in calculating the overall grade.

How overall grade is determined

You will be awarded an overall qualification grade (Distinction, Merit, and Pass). If you do not achieve the qualification you will not receive a qualification certificate, and the grade will be shown as unclassified.

The marks of each assessment will be converted into a percentage mark and rounded up or down to the nearest whole number. This percentage mark is then weighted according to the weighting of the unit assessment or synoptic assessment within the qualification. The resulting weighted assessment percentages are combined to arrive at a percentage mark for the whole qualification.

Grade definition	Percentage threshold
Distinction	90–100%
Merit	80–89%
Pass	70–79%
Unclassified	0–69% Or failure to pass one or more assessment/s

Re-sits

The AAT Professional Diploma In Accounting is not subject to re-sit restrictions.

You should only be entered for an assessment when you are well prepared and you expect to pass the assessment.

AAT qualifications

The material in this book may support the following AAT qualifications:

AAT Professional Diploma in Accounting Level 4 and AAT Professional Diploma in Accounting at SCQF Level 8.

Supplements

From time to time we may need to publish supplementary materials to one of our titles. This can be for a variety of reasons. From a small change in the AAT unit guidance to new legislation coming into effect between editions.

You should check our supplements page regularly for anything that may affect your learning materials. All supplements are available free of charge on our supplements page on our website at:

www.bpp.com/learning-media/about/students

Improving material and removing errors

There is a constant need to update and enhance our study materials in line with both regulatory changes and new insights into the assessments.

From our team of authors BPP appoints a subject expert to update and improve these materials for each new edition.

Their updated draft is subsequently technically checked by another author and from time to time non-technically checked by a proof reader.

We are very keen to remove as many numerical errors and narrative typos as we can but given the volume of detailed information being changed in a short space of time we know that a few errors will sometimes get through our net.

We apologise in advance for any inconvenience that an error might cause. We continue to look for new ways to improve these study materials and would welcome your suggestions. If you have any comments about this book, please email nisarahmed@bpp.com or write to Nisar Ahmed, AAT Head of Programme, BPP Learning Media Ltd, BPP House, Aldine Place, London W12 8AA.

Question Bank

Chapter 1 – Costing techniques

Task 1.1

At a production level of 16,000 units the production cost incurred totals £54,400. At a production level of 22,000 units the same cost totals £68,200.

This is a variable cost. True or false? Tick the correct box.

	✓
True	
False	

Task 1.2

The following details are available for four types of costs at two activity levels:

Cost type	Cost at 1,000 units £	Cost at 1,500 units £
I	7,000	10,500
II	11,000	12,500
III	12,000	12,000
IV	3,800	5,700

Complete the table to classify each cost by behaviour.

Cost	Behaviour
Cost I	
Cost II	
Cost III	
Cost IV	

Task 1.3

A manufacturing business anticipates that its variable costs and fixed costs will be £32,000 and £25,000 respectively at a production level of 10,000 units.

Complete the table to show the total production cost and the cost per unit at each of the activity levels. Show the cost per unit to THREE decimal places.

Activity level Units	Total production cost £	Cost per unit £
8,000		
12,000		
15,000		

Task 1.4

The costs of a supervisor at a manufacturing company are £20,000. One supervisor is required per 750 units produced.

Complete the table to show the total supervisors cost and the supervisors cost per unit at each of the activity levels. Show the cost per unit to TWO decimal places.

Activity level Units	Total supervisors cost £	Supervisors cost per unit £
500		
1,000		
1,500		

Task 1.5

Given below are a number of types of cost. Classify each one according to its behaviour.

	Cost behaviour
Maintenance department costs which are made up of £25,000 of salaries and an average of £500 cost per call out	
Machinery depreciation based upon machine hours used	
Salary costs of nursery school teachers, where one teacher is required for every six children in the nursery	
Rent for a building that houses the factory, stores and maintenance departments	

Task 1.6

A business produces one product which requires the following inputs:

Direct materials	6 kg @ £4.80 per kg
Direct labour	4 hours @ £7.00 per hour
Building costs	£18,000 per quarter
Leased machines	£600 for every 500 units of production
Stores costs	£3,000 per quarter plus £3.00 per unit

(a) Complete the table to show the total cost of production and the cost per unit at each of the quarterly production levels. Show the cost per unit to TWO decimal places.

Production level Units	Total cost of production £	Cost per unit £
1,000		
1,500		
2,000		

(b) **Explain why the cost per unit is different at each level of production.**

Task 1.7

The costs of a factory maintenance department appear to be partially dependent upon the number of machine hours operated each month. The machine hours and the maintenance department costs for the last six months are given below:

	Machine hours	Maintenance cost £
June	14,200	285,000
July	14,800	293,000
August	15,200	300,000
September	14,500	290,000
October	15,000	298,000
November	14,700	292,000

(a) **The variable cost per machine hour is** £ [ ] .

(b) **The fixed costs of the maintenance department are**

£ [ ] .

Task 1.8

The activity levels and related production costs for the last six months of 20X8 for a business have been as follows:

	Activity level Units	Production cost £
July	63,000	608,000
August	70,000	642,000
September	76,000	699,000
October	73,000	677,000
November	71,000	652,000
December	68,000	623,000

(a) **The fixed element of the production costs is**

£ [ ] .

The variable element of the production costs per unit is

£ [ ] .

(b) **Complete the table to show the estimated production costs at each of the levels of production.**

Level of production Units	Production cost £
74,000	
90,000	

(c) **Comment upon which of the two estimates of production costs calculated in (b) is likely to be most accurate and why.**

Task 1.9

The costs of the factory maintenance department for DF Ltd appear to have a variable element dependent upon the number of units produced. The fixed element of the costs steps up by £50,000 when 45,000 or more units are produced. The variable cost per unit is constant.

Production volume Units	£
40,000	205,000
48,000	279,000

(a)   **The variable element of the production costs per unit is**

£ [   ] .

(b)   **Complete the table to show the fixed costs at each of the levels of production.**

Level of production Units	Fixed cost £
40,000	
48,000	

....

Task 1.10

The costs of the factory maintenance department for JEB Ltd appear to have a variable element dependent upon the number of units produced. The fixed element of the costs steps up when 10,000 or more units are produced. At an activity level of 12,000 units, the fixed element of the cost is £15,000. The variable cost per unit is constant.

Production volume Units	£
8,000	58,000
13,000	93,000

(a)   **What would be the total cost for 9,000 units?**

£ [   ]

(b) **What would be the total cost for 11,000 units?**

£ [   ]

Task 1.11

The costs of the factory maintenance department for HM Ltd appear to have a variable element dependent upon the number of units produced. The fixed element of the costs steps up when 20,000 or more units are produced. The variable cost per unit is constant at £25.

Production volume Units	£
18,000	468,000
22,000	570,000

(a) **What would be the total cost for 19,000 units?**

£ [   ]

(b) **What would be the total cost for 21,000 units?**

£ [   ]

Task 1.12

A company budgeted to produce 55,000 units with fixed production costs of £233,750. The actual volume of production was 57,000 units and the actual fixed costs were £241,000.

Complete the following sentence.

The fixed production overheads were [▼] by £ [   ].

Picklist:

over-absorbed
under-absorbed

Task 1.13

The budgeted overheads of a manufacturing business have been allocated and apportioned to the two production cost centres as follows:

Cutting   £58,600
Finishing   £42,400

The two production cost centres are budgeted to produce 10,000 units in the next period.

You are also provided with the following further information:

	Cutting	Finishing
Direct labour hours	4,000	24,000
Machine hours	12,000	2,000
Direct labour cost	£24,500	£168,000
Direct materials cost	£180,000	£25,000
Prime cost	£204,500	£193,000

Complete the following table to calculate overhead absorption rates for each of the two production cost centres. Choose from the picklist when each absorption rate would be appropriate. Give your answers to TWO decimal places.

Absorption rate method	Cutting rate £	Finishing rate £	Most appropriate 1, 2 or 3
Rate per unit			▼
Rate per direct labour hour			▼
Rate per machine hour			▼

Picklist:

1   Most appropriate in a largely mechanised department where most of the overhead relates to machinery costs.

2   Most appropriate where all products are of similar size and require a similar input in terms of time and resources of the departments.

3   Most appropriate in labour intensive departments where most of the overhead relates to labour.

Task 1.14

The budgeted overheads apportioned to a business's two production cost centres, C and D, together with the budgeted labour hours and machine hours, are given below:

	C	D
Overheads	£125,000	£180,000
Direct labour hours	12,000	80,000
Machine hours	100,000	10,000

Production cost centre C is a highly mechanised department with only a few machine operatives whereas production cost centre D is a highly labour intensive department.

(a) **Complete the table to calculate separate departmental overhead absorption rates for each production cost centre using an appropriate basis.**

Department	Overhead absorption rate £
C	
D	

(b) Each unit of Product P spends the following hours in each production department:

	C	D
Direct labour hours	1	7
Machine hours	5	2

The overhead to be included in the cost of each unit of product

P is £ [   ] .

....

Task 1.15

The costs of the canteen department of a manufacturing business are estimated to be £20,000 for the following quarter. Both the packaging and assembly departments use the canteen. They have 20 and 30 employees respectively, but 50% of the assembly department work nights, when the canteen is not open. The packaging department employees do not work nights.

Complete the table below to show how much canteen overhead will be apportioned to each of the packaging and assembly departments.

	£
Overhead apportioned to packaging department	
Overhead apportioned to assembly department	

Task 1.16

In each of the following situations calculate any under- or over-absorption of overheads and state whether this would be a debit or a credit in the statement of profit or loss (income statement):

	Under-absorption £	Over-absorption £	Debit/Credit
Budgeted production was 1,200 units and budgeted overheads were £5,400. Overheads are to be absorbed on a unit basis. The actual production was 1,000 units and the overheads incurred were £5,000.			
Budgeted production was 600 units to be produced in 1,800 labour hours. Budgeted overheads of £5,040 are to be absorbed on a direct labour hour basis. The actual production for the period was 700 units in 2,200 labour hours and the actual overheads were £5,100.			

	Under-absorption £	Over-absorption £	Debit/Credit
Budgeted production was 40,000 units and the budgeted machine hours were 2 hours per unit. Budgeted overheads were £320,000 and were to be absorbed on a machine hour basis. The actual overheads incurred were £320,000 and the production was 42,000 units. The total machine hours were 82,000.			

Task 1.17

A business produces a single product in its factory which has two production departments, cutting and finishing. In the following quarter it is anticipated that 120,000 units of the product will be produced. The expected costs are:

Direct materials	£12 per unit
Direct labour	2 hours cutting @ £7.40 per hour
	1 hour finishing @ £6.80 per hour
Variable overheads Cutting	£336,000
Finishing	£132,000
Fixed overheads Cutting	£144,000
Finishing	£96,000

Overheads are absorbed on the basis of direct labour hours.

The unit cost under absorption costing will be £ [   ].

The unit cost under marginal costing will be £ [   ].

Task 1.18

Given below are the budgeted production and sales figures for the single product that a business makes and sells for the months of July and August.

	July	August
Production	24,000 units	24,000 units
Sales	22,000 units	25,000 units

There was inventory of 1,500 units of the product at the start of July.

The expected production costs for each of the two months are as follows:

Direct materials	£6.80 per unit
Direct labour	£3.60 per unit
Variable production costs	£32,400
Fixed production costs	£44,400

Overheads are absorbed on the basis of the budgeted production level and the product is sold for £16 per unit.

(a) **The absorption costing profit for July was** £ _____ .

The absorption costing profit for August was £ _____ .

The marginal costing profit for July was £ _____ .

The marginal costing profit for August was £ _____ .

(b) **Prepare a reconciliation explaining any difference in the two profit figures in each of the two months.**

Task 1.19

You are given the budgeted data about the production of a business's single product for the following quarter:

Opening inventory	840 units
Production	8,000 units
Sales	8,200 units
Direct materials	£23.60
Direct labour	4 hours @ £5.80 per hour
Variable overheads	£88,000
Fixed overheads	£51,200

Overheads are absorbed on the basis of units of production. The product has a selling price of £70 per unit.

(a) **The profit for the quarter under absorption costing is**

£ [   ] .

The profit for the quarter under marginal costing is

£ [   ] .

(b) **Prepare a reconciliation explaining any difference in the profit using absorption costing and profit using marginal costing.**

[   ]

Chapter 2 – Statistical techniques

Task 2.1

Given below are the production cost figures for the last ten months.

Calculate a three-month moving average for these figures. Give your answer to the nearest whole £.

	Production costs £	Three-month moving total £	Three-month moving average £
March	104,500		
April	110,300		
May	112,800		
June	109,400		
July	117,600		
August	116,000		
September	119,200		
October	122,300		
November	120,500		
December	119,300		

Task 2.2

A new restaurant has recently been opened which only trades for five days a week. The takings have been increasing rapidly over the first four weeks since opening, as given in the following table.

(a) **Complete the table to calculate the five-day moving average and the daily seasonal variations in accordance with the additive model.**

		Actual £	Five-day moving average – trend £	Seasonal variation (actual – trend) £
Week 1	Day 1	600		
	Day 2	700		
	Day 3	1,000		
	Day 4	1,200		
	Day 5	1,500		
Week 2	Day 1	680		
	Day 2	750		
	Day 3	1,250		
	Day 4	1,400		
	Day 5	1,860		
Week 3	Day 1	820		
	Day 2	1,030		
	Day 3	1,940		
	Day 4	2,100		
	Day 5	2,500		
Week 4	Day 1	1,000		
	Day 2	1,320		
	Day 3	1,560		
	Day 4	2,290		
	Day 5	2,670		

(b) **Write a memo to a colleague commenting upon how useful the trend and seasonal variation figures might be in this situation for forecasting future restaurant takings.**

MEMO

To: Colleague
From: Accounting technician
Date: 7 August 20X5
Subject: Usefulness of trend and seasonal variation figures

Trend

Seasonal variation

Task 2.3

Given below are the quarterly sales figures for a small business.

Complete the table to calculate the trend using a four-month centred moving average and the seasonal variations using the additive model. Give your answers to the nearest whole £.

		Actual £	Four-quarter moving average £	Centred moving average – trend £	Seasonal variations (actual – trend) £
20X5	Quarter 3	50,600			
	Quarter 4	52,800			

		Actual £	Four-quarter moving average £	Centred moving average – trend £	Seasonal variations (actual – trend) £
20X6	Quarter 1	55,600			
	Quarter 2	48,600			
	Quarter 3	51,200			
	Quarter 4	53,900			
20X7	Quarter 1	58,000			
	Quarter 2	49,800			
	Quarter 3	53,000			
	Quarter 4	54,600			
20X8	Quarter 1	60,100			
	Quarter 2	50,700			
	Quarter 3	54,200			
	Quarter 4	55,200			

Task 2.4

A business uses time series analysis and has found that the predicted trend of sales for the next four quarters and historical seasonal variations are as follows:

	Predicted trend £	Seasonal variation £
Quarter 1	418,500	+21,500
Quarter 2	420,400	+30,400
Quarter 3	422,500	–16,700
Quarter 4	423,800	–35,200

What are the predicted actual sales figures for these four quarters?

	Predicted sales £
Quarter 1	
Quarter 2	
Quarter 3	
Quarter 4	

Task 2.5

Given below are the production cost figures for a business and the retail price index (RPI) for the last six months.

(a) **Complete the table to show the production cost figures in terms of January's prices. Give your answers to the nearest whole £.**

	Actual costs £	RPI	Workings	Costs at January prices £
January	129,600	171.1		
February	129,700	172.0		
March	130,400	172.2		
April	131,600	173.0		
May	130,500	174.1		
June	131,600	174.3		

(b) Complete the table to show the production cost figures in terms of June's prices. Give your answers to the nearest whole £.

	Actual costs £	RPI	Workings	Costs at June prices £
January	129,600	171.1		
February	129,700	172.0		
March	130,400	172.2		
April	131,600	173.0		
May	130,500	174.1		
June	131,600	174.3		

(c) Write a memo to a colleague explaining what the adjusted figures in part (a) and (b) mean.

MEMO

To: Colleague
From: Accounting technician
Date: 7 August 20X5
Subject: What the adjusted figures mean

Cost figures in terms of January prices

Cost figures in terms of June prices

Task 2.6

Given below are the quarterly sales figures for a business for the last two years.

Complete the table in order to calculate an index for these sales with quarter 1 20X7 as the base period. Give your answers to ONE decimal place.

		Actual sales £	Workings	Index
20X7	Quarter 1	126,500		
	Quarter 2	130,500		
	Quarter 3	131,400		
	Quarter 4	132,500		
20X8	Quarter 1	133,100		
	Quarter 2	135,600		
	Quarter 3	136,500		
	Quarter 4	137,100		

Task 2.7

AB Ltd set the standard cost of material C at £3.50 per litre when an index of material prices stood at 115. The index now stands at 145.

What is the updated standard cost for material C?

Give your answer to TWO decimal places.

£	

Task 2.8

The direct materials cost for quarter 1 and quarter 2 of next year have been estimated in terms of current prices at £657,000 and £692,500 respectively. The current price index for these materials is 126.4 and the price index is estimated as 128.4 for quarter 1 of next year and 131.9 for quarter 2.

What are the forecast direct materials costs for quarters 1 and 2 of next year?

Give your answers to the nearest whole £.

Quarter 1	£	

Quarter 2	£	

Task 2.9

You have been given an equation and information to estimate the cost of a raw material for January and February 20X9.

The equation is $Y = a + bX$, where:

- X is the time period in months
- The value for X in November 20X8 is 29
- The value for X in December 20X8 is 30
- Y is the cost of the raw material
- The constant 'a' is 9 and constant 'b' is 0.1

Complete the table to calculate the expected price of the raw material per kilogram for January and February 20X9. Give your answer to TWO decimal places.

	£
January 20X9	
February 20X9	

Task 2.10

The total production cost varies linearly with the volume of production, and so can be described by the linear regression equation:

$y = a + bx$

Where x is the volume of production.

If the total production cost of 100 units is £2,500, and the total production cost of 1,000 units is £7,000, what are the values of a and b?

a is £ [ ]

b is £ [ ]

The total production cost for 750 units is £ [ ] .

Task 2.11

The linear regression equation for production costs for a business is:

y = 138,000 + 6.4x

Where x is the number of units.

If production is expected to be 105,000 units in the next quarter the anticipated production costs are £ [ ] .

Task 2.12

The linear regression equation for the power costs of a factory is given as follows:

y = 80,000 + 0.5x

Where x is the number of machine hours used in a period.

The anticipated machine hours for April are 380,000 hours.

The anticipated power costs for April are £ [ ] .

Task 2.13

The linear regression equation for the trend of sales in 1000s of units per month based upon time series analysis of the figures for the last two years is:

y = 3.1 + 0.9x

What is the estimated sales trend for each of the first three months of Year 3?

Month 1 = [ ] units

Month 2 = [ ] units

Month 3 = [ ] units

Task 2.14

A time series analysis of sales volumes each quarter for the last three years, 20X6 to 20X8, has identified the trend equation as follows:

$y = 400 + 105x$

Where y is the sales volume and x is the time period.

The seasonal variations for each quarter have been calculated as:

Quarter 1	−175
Quarter 2	+225
Quarter 3	+150
Quarter 4	−200

Estimate the actual sales volume for each quarter of 20X9.

Quarter 1 = [   ] units

Quarter 2 = [   ] units

Quarter 3 = [   ] units

Quarter 4 = [   ] units

Task 2.15

You have been given an equation and information to estimate the cost of raw materials for the coming two months.

The equation is $y = a + bx$, where:

- x is the time period in months
- The value for x in May 20X8 is 25
- y is the cost of raw materials
- The constant 'a' is 125 and constant 'b' is 2

The cost of raw materials is set on the first day of each month and is not changed during the month. The cost of the raw materials in May 20X8 was £175 per tonne.

(a) Calculate the expected price of the raw material per tonne for June and July 20X8.

	£
June cost per tonne	
July cost per tonne	

(b) **Convert the raw materials prices per tonne for June and July to index numbers using May 20X8 as the base (correct to two decimal places).**

June index	
July index	

Task 2.16

The relationship between distribution costs (y) and output of production and sales (x) can be described by the equation:

$y = a + bx$

You are given the following distribution costs at two different levels of output:

Output (x)	Distribution costs (y)
1,500	14,500
3,000	19,000

(a) **Calculate the values of a and b, using the two activity levels.**

	£
a	
b	

(b) **Use the values of a and b in the equation to determine the distribution costs at the following activity levels.**

Output	£
2,000 units	
4,000 units	

(c) **Complete the following sentence:**

The value of distribution costs for [▼] units is most accurate.

Picklist:

2,000
4,000

Task 2.17

The cost per kilogram for a raw material used in the production of product TNG for the last three months is shown below:

Month	Actual price £	Seasonally adjusted price £
1	985	1,040
2	1,223	1,015
3	1,150	990

(a) Complete the sentences below:

The trend in prices is [▼] of £ [   ]

per month.

The seasonal variation for month 1 is [▼] of

£ [   ] .

Picklist:

a decrease
an increase

Production costs for product MIN2 are semi-variable. The company uses the regression equation $y = a + bx$ to forecast costs where:

y = total costs
x = units
a = fixed element
b = variable element

Data has been gathered on previous costs:

Units (x)	Total cost (y) £
8,000	52,000
12,000	72,000
13,500	79,500

(b) **Using the data provided and the regression equation, calculate the values of a and b.**

a = £ [   ]

b = £ [   ]

A labour rate index is used to forecast labour costs. The index base was set when the hourly rate was £12.

(c) **Complete the table below to forecast the hourly labour rate for each month to the nearest penny.**

Month	Index number	Forecast hourly rate £
March	103.9	
April	105.2	
May	105.7	

(d) **Based on your calculations in part (c), forecast the total labour cost for April assuming that 1,920 hours are worked.**

The forecast total labour cost for April is £ [   ] .

Chapter 3 – Standard costing

Task 3.1

XYZ Ltd is planning to make 120,000 units per period of a new product. The following standards have been set:

	Per unit
Direct material A	1.2 kgs at £11 per kg
Direct material B	4.7 kgs at £6 per kg
Direct labour: Operation 1	42 minutes
Operation 2	37 minutes
Operation 3	11 minutes

Overheads are absorbed at the rate of £30 per labour hour. All direct operatives are paid at the rate of £8 per hour.

What is the standard cost of one unit?

	✓
£41.40	
£53.40	
£83.40	
£98.40	

Task 3.2

The budgeted and actual results for the month of June 20X1 are as follows:

		Budget		Actual
Production (units of XX6)		14,000		13,500
Direct materials	17,500 L	£28,875	16,800 L	£106,000
Direct labour	3,500 hours	£59,500	3,650 hours	£65,700
Fixed overheads (absorbed on a unit basis)		£77,000		£79,500
Total		£165,375		£251,200

Complete the standard cost card for the production of one unit of XX6 to TWO decimal places (dp).

One unit of XX6	Quantity	Cost per unit £	Total £
Materials			
Labour			
Fixed overheads			
Total			

Task 3.3

The budgeted and actual results for the month of June 20X1 are as follows:

		Budget		Actual
Production (units of X07)		14,000		13,500
Direct materials	17,500 litres	£28,875	16,800 litres	£106,000
Direct labour	3,500 hours	£59,500	3,650 hours	£65,700
Fixed overheads (absorbed on a unit basis)		£77,000		£79,500
Total		£165,375		£251,200

Complete the following sentences:

(a) The standard quantity of labour per unit is [   ] minutes.

(b) The budgeted quantity of materials needed to produce 13,500 units of X07 is [   ] litres.

(c) The budgeted labour hours to produce 12,000 units of X07 is [   ] hours.

(d) The budgeted labour cost to produce 13,500 units of X07 is

£ [   ] .

(e) **The budgeted overhead absorption rate per unit is**

£ [   ] .

A company budgeted to produce 25,000 units with fixed production costs of £436,250. The actual volume of production was 27,000 units and the actual fixed costs were £475,230.

(f) **The fixed production overheads were** [▼] **by**

£ [   ] .

Picklist:

over-absorbed
under-absorbed

Task 3.4

The following information has been calculated for one unit of product, Plate:

- Each unit requires 2 litres of material at a cost of £3.50 per litre.
- Each unit requires 0.5 hours of grade A labour at £15 per hour, and 0.25 hours of grade B labour at £10 per hour.
- Fixed production overheads are £100,000 and budgeted output is 20,000 units.

Complete the standard cost card.

Standard cost card for per unit of Plate	£
Direct materials	
Direct labour – grade A	
Direct labour – grade B	
Fixed overhead	
Total standard cost per unit	

Chapter 4 – Variance analysis

Task 4.1

A business budgeted to produce 2,680 units of one of its products during the month of May. The product uses 5 kg of raw material with a standard cost of £4.00 per kg. During the month the actual production was 2,800 units using 14,400 kg of raw materials costing £60,480.

Calculate the following variances:

	Variance £	Adverse/Favourable
Total materials cost variance		
Materials price variance		
Materials usage variance		

Task 4.2

A business has the following standard cost card for one unit of its product:

Direct materials	4 kg @ £3 per kg	£12
Direct labour	3 hours @ £9 per hour	£27
Fixed overheads	3 hours @ £4 per hour	£12

The budgeted production level is 12,000 units.

The actual results for the period are:

Production	11,400 units
Materials 44,800 kgs	£150,480

Calculate the following variances:

	Variance £	Adverse/Favourable
Total materials cost variance		
Materials price variance		
Materials usage variance		

Task 4.3

Production of product Z1 for the month of November in a manufacturing business was 12,100 units using 54,900 hours of direct labour costing £410,200. The standard cost card shows that the standard labour input for a unit of Z1 is 4.5 hours at a rate of £7.30 per hour.

Calculate the following variances:

	Variance £	Adverse/Favourable
Total labour cost variance		
Labour rate variance		
Labour efficiency variance		

Task 4.4

Production of product X for the month of January was 10,680 units using 53,600 hours of direct labour costing £531,800. The standard cost card shows that the standard labour input for a unit of X is 5 hours at a rate of £10 per hour.

Calculate the following variances:

	Variance £	Adverse/Favourable
Total labour cost variance		
Labour rate variance		
Labour efficiency variance		

Task 4.5

A business expects to produce 200 units of its product in 20X3. In fact 260 units were produced. The standard labour cost per unit was £70 (10 hours at a rate of £7 per hour). The actual labour cost was £18,600 and the labour force worked 2,200 hours although they were paid for 2,300 hours.

BPP
LEARNING MEDIA

Calculate the following variances:

	Variance £	Adverse/Favourable
Direct labour rate		
Direct labour efficiency		
Idle time		

Task 4.6

A business has the following standard cost card for one unit of its product:

Direct materials	4 kg @ £3 per kg	£12
Direct labour	3 hours @ £9 per hour	£27
Fixed overheads	3 hours @ £4 per hour	£12

The actual results for the period are:

Labour 34,700 hours	£347,000

A machine breakdown resulted in idle time of 300 hours.

Calculate the following variance:

	Variance £	Adverse/Favourable
Idle time variance		

Task 4.7

A business has the following standard cost card for one unit of its product:

Direct materials	4 kg @ £3 per kg	£12
Direct labour	3 hours @ £9 per hour	£27
Fixed overheads	3 hours @ £4 per hour	£12

The budgeted production level is 12,000 units.

The actual results for the period are:

Production	11,400 units
Labour 34,700 hours	£316,400

Calculate the following variances:

	Variance £	Adverse/Favourable
Total labour cost variance		
Labour rate variance		
Labour efficiency variance		

Task 4.8

A business has budgeted to produce and sell 10,000 units of its single product. The standard cost per unit is as follows:

Direct materials	£18
Direct labour	£13
Fixed production overhead	£7

During the period the actual results were:

Production and sales	11,500 units
Fixed production overheads	£75,000

The fixed overhead expenditure variance is £ [   ] .

The fixed overhead volume variance is £ [   ] .

Task 4.9

Division A manufactures a product into which fixed overheads are absorbed on the basis of labour hours. The standard cost card shows that fixed overheads are to be absorbed on the basis of 6 labour hours per unit at a rate of £7.60 per hour. The budgeted level of production is 50,000 units.

The actual results for the period showed that fixed overheads were £2,200,000, the actual hours worked were 310,000 and the actual units produced were 52,000.

Division B manufactured a product that generated an adverse material usage variance of £9,450 and a favourable material price variance of £13,520. The standard cost card states that each production unit should use 2.75kg of material at a cost of £5.40 per kg. The actual cost of material was £515,680.

Calculate the following:

		Adverse/Favourable
Division A Fixed overhead expenditure variance (£)		
Division A Fixed overhead volume variance (£)		
Division B Total materials used (kg)		
Division B Material usage variance (kg)		

Task 4.10

A business incurred fixed overheads of £203,000 in the month of May. The fixed overheads are absorbed into units of production at the rate of £3.60 per direct labour hour. The actual production during the month was 13,200 units although the budget had been for 14,000 units. The standard labour cost for the production is 4 hours per unit at an hourly rate of £8.00. During the month 50,000 labour hours were worked at a total cost of £403,600.

Calculate the following figures:

(a) The budgeted fixed overhead for the month was

£ [ ] .

(b) The fixed overhead expenditure variance was

£ [ ] .

(c) The fixed overhead volume variance was £ [ ] .

Another business generated a £13,600 adverse labour efficiency variance in June. Actual production was 25,650 units. Standard labour hours per unit are 2 hours, and the standard cost per hour is £8.

(d) The labour efficiency variance in hours for June was [ ] .

(e) The number of labour hours worked in June [ ] hours.

Task 4.11

You are employed as part of the management accounting team in a large industrial company which operates a four-weekly system of management reporting. Your division makes a single product, the Omega, and, because of the nature of the production process, there is no work in progress at any time.

The group management accountant has completed the calculation of the material and labour standard costing variances for the current period to 1 April but has not had the time to complete any other variances. Details of the variances already calculated are reproduced in the working papers below, along with other standard costing data.

Standard costing and budget data – four weeks ended 1 April			
	Quantity	Unit price £	Cost per unit £
Material (kg)	7	25.00	175
Labour (hours)	40	7.50	300
Fixed overheads (hours)	40	12.50	500
			975
	Units	Standard unit cost	Standard cost of production
Budgeted production for the four weeks	4,100	£975	£3,997,500

Working papers

Actual production and expenditure for the four weeks ended 1 April

Units produced	3,850
Cost of 30,000 kgs of materials consumed	£795,000
Cost of 159,000 labour hours worked	£1,225,000
Expenditure on fixed overheads	£2,195,000

Calculate the following variances:

(a)   The fixed overhead expenditure variance

(b)   The fixed overhead volume variance

Task 4.12

The variable production overhead cost of product X is as follows:

2 hours at £1.50 = £3 per unit

During period 6, 400 units of product X were made. The labour force worked 760 hours. The variable overhead cost was £1,230.

Calculate the following variances:

	Variance £	Adverse/Favourable
Total variable production overhead total variance		
Variable production overhead expenditure variance		
Variable production overhead efficiency variance		

Task 4.13

P Co, a manufacturing firm, operates a standard marginal costing system. It makes a single product, PG, using a single raw material.

Standard costs relating to PG have been calculated as follows:

Standard cost schedule – PG	Per unit £
Direct material, 100 kg at £5 per kg	500
Direct labour, 10 hours at £8 per hour	80
Variable production overhead, 10 hours at £2 per hour	20
	600

The standard selling price of a PG is £900 and P Co plan to produce and sell 1,020 units a month.

During December 20X0, 1,000 units of PG were produced and sold. Relevant details of this production are as follows.

Direct material

90,000 kgs costing £720,000 were bought and used.

Direct labour

8,200 hours were worked during the month and total wages were £63,000.

Variable production overhead

The actual cost for the month was £25,000.

(a) **The variable production cost variance for December 20X0 is**

£ _____ .

(b) (i) **The direct labour rate variance is** £ _____ .

(ii) **The direct labour efficiency variance is** £ _____ .

(c) (i) **The direct material price variance is** £ _____ .

(ii) **The direct material usage variance is** £ _____ .

(d) (i) **The variable production overhead expenditure variance is** £ _____ .

(ii) **The variable production overhead efficiency variance is**

£ _____ .

Task 4.14

A company produced 23,000 units in March and generated a material price variance of £3,800 adverse. The actual materials purchased and used were 68,000 kg, costing a total of £197,600. The material usage variance was £2,850 favourable.

Calculate the standard cost per kg of material and the standard number of kg of material per unit.

Standard cost per kg

£ ⬚ .

Standard number of kg per unit

⬚ kg.

Task 4.15

A company purchases and uses 200,000 litres of material at a cost of £0.55 per litre. The budgeted production was 22,000 units which requires 220,000 litres of material at a total standard cost of £132,000. The actual production was 19,000 units.

(a) Complete the following statement:

The material usage variance is £ ⬚ ⬚ .

Picklist:

adverse
favourable

A company expects to produce 10,000 units of X using 6,000 hours of labour. The standard cost of labour is £15 per hour. The actual output was 12,000 units. 6,900 hours of labour were worked at a total cost of £105,850.

(b) Complete the following statement:

The total labour efficiency variance is £ ⬚

⬚ .

Picklist:

adverse
favourable

Task 4.16

Bert manufactures a product, RPB. Bert operates a standard cost system in which production overheads are fixed and absorbed on a unit basis.

The budgeted activity is for the production of 28,000 units at a total fixed production cost of £350,000. The actual volume of production was 30,000 units and the fixed overhead expenditure variance was £35,000 favourable.

Complete the following sentences:

(a) The fixed overhead volume variance is £ [   ]

[▼] .

Picklist:

adverse
favourable

(b) The actual fixed production overheads incurred were

£ [   ] .

The variable production overhead cost of a product is as follows:

2 hours at £2.50 = £5 per unit

During period 3, 750 units of the product were made. The labour force worked 1,450 hours. The variable overhead cost was £3,700.

(c) **Calculate the following variances:**

Variance	Amount £	Sign
Total variable production overhead variance		▼
Variable overhead expenditure variance		▼

Picklist:

Adverse
Favourable

Task 4.17

The budgeted activity and actual results for the month of August 20X1 are as follows:

	Budget		Actual	
Production (KK1)		18,000		15,000
Direct materials	9,000 kg	£60,750	7,800 kg	£55,770
Direct labour	5,400 hours	£47,250	4,230 hours	£38,070
Fixed overheads		£76,500		£71,300
Total cost		£184,500		£165,140

Complete the following table:

Variance	Amount £	Adverse/Favourable
Direct material usage variance		▼
Direct material price variance		▼
Total direct labour variance		▼

Picklist:

Adverse
Favourable

....

Task 4.18

Albert manufactures product BRP. Albert operates a standard cost system in which production overheads are fixed and absorbed on a unit basis.

The budgeted activity and actual results for the month are as follows:

	Budget	Actual
Production units (BRP)	25,000	27,000
Fixed overheads	£1,043,750	£947,500

(a) Calculate the following variances:

Variance	Amount £	Sign
Fixed overhead expenditure		▼
Fixed overhead volume		▼

Picklist:

Adverse
Favourable

Albert decides to manufacture a new product, the ZX250. The variable production overhead cost per unit of the product is: £15 (3 hours at £5.00).

During April, 1,075 units of ZX250 were produced and 3,050 labour hours were worked. Total variable overhead cost was £15,000.

(b) Calculate the following variances:

Variance	Amount £	Sign
Variable overhead expenditure variance		▼
Variable overhead efficiency variance		▼

Picklist:

Adverse
Favourable

Task 4.19

A business has supplied you with the following information:

	£	Hours
Favourable material price variance	150	
Standard cost per kilogram of material	15	
Actual cost of material	615	
Adverse labour rate variance	360	
Actual labour hours		575
Actual cost of labour	7,835	

Complete the following sentences:

The actual quantity of material used is [   ] kg.

The standard labour rate is £ [   ] per hour.

Task 4.20

A business has supplied you with the following information:

	£	Kg
Favourable material price variance	1,370	
Actual kg used		6,850
Actual cost of materials	21,920	

Complete the following sentence:

The standard material price is £ [   ] per kg (to 2 dp).

Task 4.21

A company purchases 3,700 kilograms of material at a cost of £10,915. The total material price variance is £1,665 adverse.

Complete the following statement:

The standard cost per kilogram is £ [   ] .

Task 4.22

Delta manufactures 5,400 units of product QR1 using 11,880 labour hours. The budgeted production was 5,000 units using 11,250 labour hours at a cost of £163,125. The labour rate variance is £14,850 favourable.

Complete the following sentence:

The actual labour rate per hour is £ [   ] .

Task 4.23

The standard material content of one unit of product A is 25kgs of material X which should cost £10 per kilogram. In March 20X4, 6,250 units of product A were produced and there was an adverse material usage variance of £7,500.

Complete the following sentence:

The quantity of material X used in March 20X4 is ⬚ kg.

....

Chapter 5 – Operating statements

Task 5.1

You are employed as a management accountant in the head office of Travel Holdings plc. Travel Holdings owns a number of transport businesses. One of them is Travel Ferries Ltd. Travel Ferries operates ferries which carry passengers and vehicles across a large river. Each year, standard costs are used to develop the budget for Travel Ferries Ltd. The latest budgeted and actual operating results are reproduced below.

Travel Ferries Ltd Budgeted and actual operating results for the year to 30 November 20X8				
Operating data	**Budget**			**Actual**
Number of ferry crossings	6,480			5,760
Operating hours of ferries	7,776			7,488
Cost data	**£**			**£**
Fuel	1,244,160 litres	497,664	1,232,800 litres	567,088
Labour	93,312 hours	699,840	89,856 hours	696,384
Fixed overheads		466,560		472,440
Cost of operations		1,664,064		1,735,912

Other accounting information

- Fuel and labour are variable costs.
- Fixed overheads are absorbed on the basis of budgeted operating hours.

One of your duties is to prepare costing information and a standard costing reconciliation statement for the chief executive of Travel Holdings.

Required

(a) Calculate the following information:

    (i) **The standard price of fuel per litre**

    (ii) **The standard litres of fuel for 5,760 ferry crossings**

    (iii) **The standard labour rate per hour**

    (iv) **The standard labour hours for 5,760 ferry crossings**

(v) **The standard fixed overhead cost per budgeted operating hour**

(vi) **The standard operating hours for 5,760 crossings**

(vii) **The standard fixed overhead cost absorbed by the actual 5,760 ferry crossings**

(b) **Using the data provided in the operating results and your answers to part (a), calculate the following variances:**

(i) **The material price variance for the fuel**
(ii) **The material usage variance for the fuel**
(iii) **The labour rate variance**
(iv) **The labour efficiency variance**
(v) **The fixed overhead expenditure variance**
(vi) **The fixed overhead volume variance**

(c) **Prepare a statement reconciling the actual cost of operations to the standard cost of operations for the year to 30 November 20X8.**

Statement reconciling the actual cost of operations to the standard cost of operations for year ended 30 November 20X8

Number of ferry crossings		5,760
	£	**£**
Actual cost of operations		
Cost variances	**Adverse**	
Material price for fuel		
Material usage for fuel		
Labour rate		
Labour efficiency		
Fixed overhead expenditure		
Fixed overhead volume		
Standard cost of operations		

Task 5.2

The following budgetary control report has been provided together with the variances calculated below.

	Budget		Actual	
Production (units)		12,400		13,600
Direct materials	37,200 kg	£130,200	37,400 kg	£112,200
Direct labour	24,800 hours	£223,200	28,560 hours	£285,600
Fixed overheads		£234,000		£221,000
Total cost		£587,400		£618,800

Variance	Amount £
Direct material price	18,700 (F)
Direct materials usage	11,900 (F)
Direct labour rate	28,560 (A)
Direct labour efficiency	12,240
Fixed overhead expenditure	13,000

The company normally prepares an operating statement under standard absorption costing principles but the financial director has asked you to prepare one under standard marginal costing principles.

(a) **Select the fixed overhead volume variance from the Picklist, drag and drop the options from the Variances list into the correct spaces (Favourable or Adverse) and fill in the remaining spaces to complete the table.**

	£		£
Budgeted variable cost for actual production			
Budgeted fixed cost			
Total budgeted cost for actual production			
Variance	**Favourable £**	**Adverse £**	
Direct materials price			
Direct materials usage			
Direct labour rate			
Direct labour efficiency			
Fixed overhead expenditure			
Fixed overhead volume	▼	▼	
Total variance			
Actual cost of actual production			

Picklist for fixed overhead volume variance:

22,645.16
N/A

Drag and drop options for variances:

| £18,700 | £11,900 | £28,560 | £12,240 | £13,000 |

A company has a budgeted overhead absorption rate of £95 per unit and budgeted production of 27,000 units. The actual production was 25,000 units and the actual overheads incurred were £2,423,600.

(b) **Complete the following statement:**

The [　　　　　　　▼] of overheads is [£ 　　　　　　　] .

Picklist:

over-absorption
under-absorption

Task 5.3

A budgetary control report has been provided for the manufacture of product PD98 and variances have been calculated.

	Budget		Actual	
Production (units)		450		520
Direct materials	337.5 kg	£20,250	338 kg	£25,350
Direct labour	1,080 hours	£12,960	988 hours	£14,820
Fixed overheads		£28,080		£31,300
Total cost		£61,290		£71,470

Variance	Amount
Direct materials price	£5,070 (A)
Direct materials usage	£3,120
Fixed overhead expenditure	£3,220
Fixed overhead volume	£4,368 (F)
Direct labour rate	£2,964
Direct labour efficiency	£3,120 (F)

Complete the operating statement for the manufacture of PD98. Do not use brackets or minus signs for the variances.

			£
Budgeted/Standard cost for actual production			
Variances	**Adverse £**	**Favourable £**	
Direct material price			
Direct materials usage			
Direct labour rate			
Direct labour efficiency			
Fixed overhead expenditure			
Fixed overhead volume			
Total variance			
Actual cost of actual production			

....

Task 5.4

The standard cost card for a business's product is shown below:

	£
Direct materials 4.8 kg at £2.80 per kg	13.44
Direct labour 2.5 hours at £8.50 per hour	21.25
Fixed overheads 2.5 hours at £1.60 per hour	4.00
	38.69

The budgeted production was for 1,100 units in the month of July. The actual costs during the month of July for the production of 1,240 units were as follows:

	£
Direct materials 5,800 kg	17,100
Direct labour 3,280 hours	27,060
Fixed overheads	4,650

The following variances have been calculated:

Variances	£
Materials price	860 (A)
Materials usage	426 (F)
Labour rate	820 (F)
Labour efficiency	1,530 (A)
Fixed overhead expenditure	250 (A)
Fixed overhead volume	560 (F)

Calculate the budgeted cost of 1,240 units of production and insert the variances in the correct place in the following operating statement. Total the variances and reconcile the budgeted cost of actual production to the actual cost of actual production.

			£
Budgeted cost of actual production			
Variances	**Favourable £**	**Adverse £**	
Materials price			
Materials usage			
Labour rate			
Labour efficiency			
Fixed overhead expenditure			
Fixed overhead volume			
Total variances			
Actual cost of actual production			

Task 5.5

Bedworth Co has the following cost card for unit of product C:

Direct materials	5kg @ £2 per kg	£10
Direct labour	2 hours @ £8 per hour	£16
Fixed overheads	2 hours @ £4 per hour	£8

The budgeted level of production is 12,000 units. The actual results for the period are:

Production	11,400 units
Materials	45,600 kg costing £136,800
Labour	11,400 hours costing £79,800
Fixed overheads	£95,000

(a) Prepare a reconciliation of the budgeted material cost with the actual material cost using the material cost variances.

			£
Standard cost of materials for actual production			
Variances	**Favourable £**	**Adverse £**	
Direct material price variance			
Direct material usage variance			
Total variance			
Actual cost of materials for actual production			

(b) Prepare a reconciliation of the budgeted labour cost with the actual labour cost using the labour cost variances.

			£
Standard cost of labour for actual production			
Variances	**Favourable £**	**Adverse £**	
Direct labour rate variance			
Direct labour efficiency variance			
Total variance			
Actual cost of labour for actual production			

(c) Prepare a reconciliation of the budgeted fixed overhead cost with the actual fixed overhead cost using the fixed overhead cost variances.

			£
Standard cost of fixed overhead for actual production			
Variances	**Favourable £**	**Adverse £**	
Fixed overhead expenditure variance			
Fixed overhead volume variance			
Total variance			
Actual cost of fixed overhead for actual production			

Task 5.6

You are employed as the assistant management accountant in the group accountant's office of Hampstead plc. Hampstead recently acquired Finchley Ltd, a small company making a specialist product called the Alpha. Standard marginal costing is used by all the companies within the group and, from 1 August 20X8, Finchley Ltd will also be required to use standard marginal costing in its management reports. Part of your job is to manage the implementation of standard marginal costing at Finchley Ltd.

John Wade, the managing director of Finchley, is not clear how the change will help him as a manager. He has always found Finchley's existing absorption costing system sufficient. By way of example, he shows you a summary of his management accounts for the three months to 31 May 20X8. These are reproduced below.

Statement of budgeted and actual cost of Alpha production – 3 months ended 31 May 20X8					
	Actual		**Budget**		**Variance**
Alpha production (units)		10,000		12,000	
	Inputs	**£**	**Inputs**	**£**	**£**
Materials	32,000 m	377,600	36,000 m	432,000	54,400
Labour	70,000 hrs	422,800	72,000 hrs	450,000	27,200
Fixed overhead absorbed		330,000		396,000	66,000
Fixed overhead unabsorbed		75,000		0	(75,000)
		1,205,400		1,278,000	72,600

John Wade is not convinced that standard marginal costing will help him to manage Finchley. 'My current system tells me all I need to know,' he said. 'As you can see, we are £72,600 below budget which is really excellent given that we lost production as a result of a serious machine breakdown.'

To help John Wade understand the benefits of standard marginal costing, you agree to prepare a statement for the three months ended 31 May 20X8 reconciling the standard cost of production to the actual cost of production.

Required

Write a short memo to John Wade:

Your memo should:

(i)   **Use the budget data to determine the following:**

     (1)   **The standard marginal cost per Alpha**

     (2)   **The standard marginal cost of actual Alpha production for the three months to 31 May 20X8**

(ii)   **Calculate the following variances:**

     (1)   **Material price variance**
     (2)   **Material usage variance**
     (3)   **Labour rate variance**
     (4)   **Labour efficiency variance**
     (5)   **Fixed overhead expenditure variance**

(iii)   **Include a statement reconciling the actual cost of production to the standard cost of production**

(iv)   **Give TWO reasons why your variances might differ from those in his original management accounting statement, despite using the same basic data**

(v)   **Briefly discuss ONE further reason why your reconciliation statement provides improved management information**

MEMO

To: Managing Director
From: Assistant Management Accountant
Date: xx/xx/xx

Subject: The use of standard marginal costing at Finchley Ltd

(i) (1) **Standard marginal cost of a unit of Alpha**

(2) **Standard cost of producing 10,000 units of Alpha**

(ii) **Variance calculations:**

(1) Material price variance
(2) Material usage variance
(3) Labour rate variance
(4) Labour efficiency variance
(5) Fixed overhead expenditure variance

(iii) **Reconciliation statement**

			£
Standard cost of output			
Variances	**Fav £**	**Adv £**	
Materials price			
Materials usage			
Labour rate			
Labour efficiency			
Fixed overhead expenditure			
Total variance			
Actual cost of output			

Task 5.7

The following budgetary control report has been provided:

	Budget		Actual	
Units	1,100		1,240	
Material	5,280 litres	£14,784	5,800 litres	£17,100
Labour	2,750 hours	£23,375	3,280 hours	£27,060
Fixed overheads		£4,400		£4,650
Total cost		£42,559		£48,810

The following variances have been calculated:

	£
Fixed overhead expenditure	250
Direct materials price	860 (A)
Direct materials usage	426
Direct labour rate	820
Direct labour efficiency	1,530 (A)
Fixed overhead volume	560 (F)

Complete the operating statement:

			£
Budgeted/Standard cost for actual production			
Variances	**Favourable £**	**Adverse £**	
Direct materials price			
Direct materials usage			
Direct labour rate			
Direct labour efficiency			
Fixed overhead expenditure			
Fixed overhead volume			
Total variance			
Actual cost of actual production			

Chapter 6 – Interpreting variances

Task 6.1

State possible reasons for each of the following variances which are all independent of each other.

Variance	Possible causes
Favourable materials price variance	
Favourable materials usage variance	
Adverse labour rate variance	
Adverse labour efficiency variance	

Task 6.2

What possible effect will the following scenarios have on the variances?

Scenario	Possible effects
A business has had to use a less-skilled grade of labour in its production process	
A factory had a machine breakdown which resulted in three days of production delays last month	

Task 6.3

The standard direct materials cost for a business's product is:

6 kg @ £8.00 per kg = £48.00

During the month of October production was 7,400 units of the product and the actual materials cost was £397,400 for 45,100 kgs. The price of the materials has been unexpectedly increased to £8.50 per kg for the whole month.

The total materials price variance is £ [   ].

The non-controllable element of the materials price variance that has been caused by the price increase is £ [   ].

The controllable element of the materials price variance caused by other factors is £ [   ].

Task 6.4

A business's product has a standard direct material cost of £26.00 (4 kg @ £6.50 per kg). During the month of March the total production of the product was 2,500 units using 10,600 kg of materials at a total cost of £73,140. During the month the price was unexpectedly increased due to a shortage of the material to £7.00 per kg.

The total materials price variance is £ [   ].

The non-controllable variance due to price increase is £ [   ].

The controllable variance due to other factors is £ [   ].

Task 6.5

A business makes a product which uses a raw material which has a standard cost of £7.00 per kg. The standard hasn't been updated for a while. Each unit of the product requires 5 kg of this material. The price of the materials for the last few years has been subjected to a time series analysis and the following seasonal variations have been seen to occur.

Jan – Mar	–£0.42
Apr – June	+£0.56
July – Aug	+£0.77
Sept – Dec	–£0.91

During March 18,000 units of the product were made and the price paid for the 92,000 kg of material was £631,200.

The total materials price variance is £ [   ].

The non-controllable variance due to the season is £ [   ].

The controllable variance due to other factors is £ [   ].

Task 6.6

The standard cost of direct materials for a product is made up of 8 kg of material at an average standard cost of £4.00 per kg. It has been noted over the years that the cost of the material fluctuates on a seasonal basis around the average standard cost as follows:

Jan – Mar	+£0.48
Apr – June	+£0.72
July – Sept	–£0.64
Oct – Dec	–£0.56

In the month of June the actual production was 5,000 units and 42,300 kg of material were used at a cost of £194,580.

The total materials price variance is £ _____ .

The non-controllable variance caused by the seasonal price change

is £ _____ .

The controllable variance caused by other factors is £ _____ .

Task 6.7

A business sets the standard cost of its materials at 5 kg per unit at a price of £20 per kg, when the index for this particular materials price was 120. During January, 9,000 units were produced using 46,000 kg of material at a total cost of £946,000. In January, the index of the materials price stood at 130.

The total materials price variance is £ _____ .

The non-controllable variance caused by the index change is

£ _____ .

The controllable variance caused by other factors is £ _____ .

Task 6.8

Keta operates a standard costing system and uses raw material C2X which is a global commodity. The standard price was set based upon a market price of £450 per litre when the material price index for C2X was 120.50. The following information has been gathered:

- The price index increased to 126.525 in June X3.
- The raw material price variance for June was £375,000 adverse.
- 12,500 litres of material C2X were purchased in June.

Complete the statements below. In order to calculate your answers, you should split the raw material price variance into two components by calculating the part of the variance explained by the change in the price index and the part of the variance not explained by the changes in the price index.

(a) The part of the variance explained by the increase in the price index is

£ [   ] .

(b) The part of the variance not explained by the increase in the price index is

£ [   ] .

(c) The percentage increase in the index is [   ] %.

Hamma uses product Z4QX and has collected data from the last few months in order to forecast the cost per kilogram of Z4QX in the next period.

	April X3	May X3	June X3
Cost per kilogram of Z4QX (£)	1,457.92	1,593.66	1,729.40

(d) **Complete the table below to forecast the expected price of product Z4QX in September and December X3 (to two dp).**

	September X3	December X3
Cost per kilogram of Z4QX (£)		

A colleague has calculated the regression line (the line of best fit) as **y = 24.69 + 2.14x**, where y is the cost per kilogram and x is the period. June X3 is period 41.

(e) **Complete the statement below:**

The forecast cost per kilogram, using the regression line, for September X3 is

£ [   ] .

....

Task 6.9

Croxton Ltd makes a specialised chemical, X14, in barrels at its factory. The factory has two departments: the processing department and the finishing department. Because of the technology involved, Croxton apportions both budgeted and actual total factory fixed overheads between the two departments on the basis of budgeted machine hours.

The standard absorption cost per barrel of X14 in the processing department, and the budgeted production for the five weeks ended 31 May 20X8, are shown below.

Processing department: standard cost per barrel of X14			
Input	Quantity	Standard price/rate	Cost £
Material	10 litres	£60 per litre	600
Labour	8 labour hrs	£8 per labour hr	64
Fixed overheads	16 machine hrs	£20 per machine hr	320
Standard absorption cost per barrel			984
Budgeted production five weeks ending 31 May 20X8			45 barrels

You are employed by Croxton Ltd as an accounting technician. One of your duties is to prepare standard costing reconciliation statements. Croxton's finance director gives you the following information for the five weeks ended 31 May 20X8.

Total factory budgeted and actual data

Factory budgeted machine hours	1,152
Factory budgeted fixed overheads	£23,040
Factory actual fixed overheads	£26,000

Budgeted **and** actual factory fixed overheads are apportioned between the processing and finishing departments **on the basis of budgeted machine hours**.

Processing department actual data

Actual costs	
Materials at £58.50 per litre	£23,985
Labour (328 hours)	£2,788
Actual production output	40 barrels
Actual machine hours worked	656

There was no work in progress at any stage.

Required

(a) Calculate the following information for the processing department:

    (i)   Actual litres of material used

    (ii)   Standard litres of material required for 40 barrels of X14

    (iii)   Average actual labour rate per hour

    (iv)   Standard labour hours required for 40 barrels of X14

    (v)   Budgeted number of machine hours

    (vi)   Budgeted fixed overheads

    (vii)   Actual fixed overheads (based on its share of actual factory overhead)

    (viii) Standard machine hours for actual production

    (ix)   Standard absorption cost of actual production

    (x)   Actual absorption cost of actual production

(b) Using data given and your answers to part (a), calculate the following variances for the processing department:

    (i)   Material price variance
    (ii)   Material usage variance
    (iii)   Labour rate variance
    (iv)   Labour efficiency variance
    (v)   Fixed overhead expenditure variance
    (vi)   Fixed overhead volume variance

(c) **Prepare a statement for the five weeks ended 31 May 20X8 reconciling the standard absorption cost of actual production with the actual absorption cost of actual production.**

			£
Standard absorption cost of actual production			
	Favourable £	**Adverse £**	
Variances			
Material price			
Material usage			
Labour rate			
Labour efficiency			
Fixed overhead expenditure			
Fixed overhead volume			
Total variances			
Actual absorption cost of actual production			

Judith Green is the production manager of the processing department. You show her the statement reconciling the actual and standard costs of actual production. Judith then gives you the following additional information:

- When the standard costs were agreed, a price index for the material used in making the X14 was 140, but during the five weeks ended 31 May it was 133.

- Actual production output was 40 barrels but Croxton had to make 41 barrels of X14 as one barrel had to be scrapped on completion. This was because the barrel was damaged. The scrapped barrel had no value.

- If labour hours worked exceed 320 hours per five weeks, overtime is incurred. The overtime premium is £8.00 per hour of overtime.

- There is just one customer for the X14. The customer purchased 40 barrels during the five weeks ended 31 May 20X8.

Judith believes there is no need to examine the variances any further, for a number of reasons.

- The material price variance clearly shows that the purchasing department is efficient.

- The labour rate, labour efficiency and material usage variances were entirely due to the one scrapped barrel.

- Fixed overheads are not controllable by the processing department.

(d) **Write a memo to Judith Green. In your memo you should do the following:**

(i) **Use the material price index to identify a revised standard price for the materials used in X14.**

(ii) **Subdivide the material price variance calculated in task (b) (i) into that part due to the change in the price index and that part due to other reasons.**

(iii) **Briefly explain whether the material price variance calculated in task (b) (i) arose from efficiencies in the purchasing department.**

(iv) **Explain whether the one scrapped barrel might fully account for the following:**

(1) **Material usage variance**
(2) **Labour efficiency variance**
(3) **Labour rate variance**

(v) **Give ONE reason why the fixed overheads might not be controllable by the processing department.**

MEMO

To: Judith Green, production manager
From: Accounting technician
Date: 7 August 20X5
Subject: Croxton Ltd – analysis of variances for five weeks ended
              31 May 20X8

Task 6.10

You are the assistant management accountant at the Bare Foot Hotel complex on the tropical island of St Nicolas. The hotel complex is a luxury development. All meals and entertainment are included in the price of the holiday and guests only have to pay for drinks.

The Bare Foot Hotel complex aims to create a relaxing atmosphere. Because of this, meals are available throughout the day and guests can eat as many times as they wish.

The draft performance report for the hotel for the seven days ended 27 November 20X8 is reproduced below:

Bare Foot Hotel Complex

Draft performance report for seven days ended 27 November 20X8

	Notes			Budget			Actual
Guests				540			648
		£		£		£	£
Variable costs							
Meal costs	1			34,020			49,896
Catering staff costs	2,3			3,780			5,280
Total variable costs				37,800			55,176
Fixed overhead costs							
Salaries of other staff		5,840				6,000	
Local taxes		4,500				4,200	
Light, heat and power		2,500				2,600	
Depreciation of buildings and equipment		5,000				4,000	
Entertainment		20,500				21,000	
Total fixed overheads				38,340			37,800
Total cost of providing for guests				76,140			92,976

Notes

1   Budgeted cost of meals: number of guests × 3 meals per day × 7 days × £3 per meal

2   Budgeted cost of catering staff: each member of the catering staff is to prepare and serve 12 meals per hour. Cost = (number of guests × 3 meals per day × 7 days ÷ 12 meals per hour) × £4 per hour.

3   Actual hours worked by catering staff = 1,200 hours

4   The amount of food per meal has been kept under strict portion control. Since preparing the draft performance report, however, it has been discovered that guests have eaten, on average, four meals per day.

You report to Alice Groves, the general manager of the hotel, who feels that the format of the draft performance report could be improved to provide her with more meaningful management information. She suggests that the budgeted and actual data given in the existing draft performance report is rearranged in the form of a standard costing report, using absorption costing.

Required

(a)   (i)   **Use the budget data, the actual data and the notes to the performance report to calculate the following for the seven days ended 27 November 20X8:**

(1)   **The actual number of meals served**

(2)   **The standard number of meals which should have been served for the actual number of guests**

(3)   **The actual hourly rate paid to catering staff**

(4)   **The standard hours allowed for catering staff to serve three meals per day for the actual number of guests**

(5)   **The standard fixed overhead per guest**

(6)   **The total standard cost for the actual number of guests**

(ii)   **Use the data given in the task and your answers to part (a) (i) to calculate the following variances for the seven days ended 27 November 20X8:**

(1)   **The material price variance for meals served**

(2)   **The material usage variance for meals served**

(3)   **The labour rate variance for catering staff**

(4) **The labour efficiency variance for catering staff, based on a standard of three meals served per guest per day**

(5) **The fixed overhead expenditure variance**

(6) **The fixed overhead volume variance on the assumption that the fixed overhead absorption rate is based on the budgeted number of guests per seven days**

(iii) **Prepare a statement reconciling the standard cost for the actual number of guests to the actual cost for the actual number of guests for the seven days ended 27 November 20X8.**

Task 6.11

You have been provided with the following information for an organisation, which manufactures a product called Becks, for the month just ended:

	Budget		Actual	
Production (units)		20,000		21,000
Direct materials	80,000 kg	£880,000	83,000 kg	£954,500

The finance director has asked you to write a note to help in the training of a junior accounting technician. The notes are to explain the calculation of the total direct material variance and how this variance can be split into a price variance and a usage variance.

Required

Prepare a note explaining the total direct material variance and how it can be split into a price variance and usage variance. Calculations should be used to illustrate the explanation.

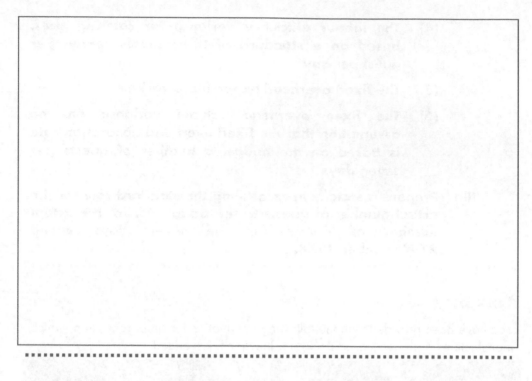

Task 6.12

You are employed as an accounting technician at BeThere Airlines, a company that operates flights across Europe. The company has several divisions including a catering division operating from Manchester. The catering division produces meals daily for the flights. Currently all meals produced are used only on BeThere flights.

The company operates an integrated standard cost system in which:

- Purchases of materials are recorded at standard cost
- Direct material costs and direct labour costs are variable
- Production overheads are fixed and absorbed using direct labour hours

The budgeted activity and actual results for November 20X6 are as follows:

		Budget		Actual
Production (meals)		112,000		117,600
Direct materials	56,000 kg	£224,000	61,740 kg	£185,220
Direct labour	28,000 hours	£252,000	27,930 hours	£279,300
Fixed overheads		£84,000		£82,000
Total cost		£560,000		£546,520

Required

(a) Calculate the following information for November (to 2 decimal places):

(i) Standard price of materials per kilogram
(ii) Standard usage of materials per meal
(iii) Standard labour rate per hour
(iv) Standard labour hours per meal
(v) Budgeted overhead absorption rate per hour
(vi) Overheads absorbed into actual production
(vii) The total standard cost of actual production

(b) Calculate the following variances for November:

(i) Direct material price variance

(ii) Direct material usage variance

(iii) Direct labour rate variance

(iv) Direct labour efficiency variance

(v) Fixed overhead expenditure variance

(vi) Fixed overhead volume variance and explain the reason for the variance

(c) Prepare a report to the managing director giving **ONE** possible reason for each of the following variances you calculated in (b).

(i) Direct material price variance
(ii) Direct material usage variance
(iii) Direct labour rate variance
(iv) Direct labour efficiency variance

REPORT

To: Managing Director
From: Accounting Technician
Subject: Reasons for the variances
Date: 14 December 20X6

Direct material price variance

Direct material usage variance

Direct labour rate variance

Direct labour efficiency variance

....

Task 6.13

You have been provided with the following operating statement for Soupzz Ltd, which produces vegetable soup using mainly carrots and potatoes:

Variances	Favourable	Adverse
Direct materials (carrots) price		£1,750
Direct materials (carrots) usage	£760	
Direct materials (potatoes) price	£450	
Direct materials (potatoes) usage		£1,700

The chef has given you the following information about the ingredients and production of the soup:

The region where Soupzz's carrot supplier is located has recently been hit by flooding which means that much of the carrot crop was destroyed. Soupzz Ltd has had to use suppliers from further afield to get the required quantity of carrots. One of these new suppliers has provided some very sweet tasting carrots with a stronger flavour and Soupzz Ltd is considering whether to change suppliers next year.

Soupzz has very little control over the price it pays for its carrots as this is dependent on the quantity and the quality of carrots produced – which is influenced by the weather.

Following some bad press about carbohydrates making people fat, general demand for potatoes has dropped and this has led to potato suppliers reducing their prices. As the carrots were sweeter, Soupzz used more potatoes and fewer carrots in its soup than usual.

There was a fault in one of the machines which took a long time to be fixed. This resulted in labour staff temporarily having nothing to do.

Required

Using this information, prepare a report to the Production Director to cover the following:

(a) **Provide possible reasons for the carrots and potatoes variances by considering the following:**

- **Price of the ingredients**
- **Quality of the ingredients**
- **Mix of ingredients**

(b) **Discuss the type of labour variance that the machine breakdown would have caused.**

To:	Subject:
From:	Date:

(a) Possible reasons for the variances:

- Direct materials (carrots) price variance

- Direct materials (carrots) usage variance

- Direct materials (potatoes) price variance

- Direct materials (potatoes) usage variance

(b) Machine downtime and labour variances

Chapter 7 – Performance indicators

Task 7.1

Suggest possible measures of productivity for each of the following types of organisation:

Organisation	Possible productivity measures
Taxi firm	
Hospital	
Motorbike courier service	
Firm of accountants	
Retail store	
Maker of hand-made pottery	

Task 7.2

You are given the following information about a small manufacturing business for the year ending 31 March:

Sales revenue	£1,447,600
Cost of materials used	£736,500
Cost of bought in services	£316,900
Number of employees	15

The total value added is £ _____ .

The value added per employee is £ _____ .

Task 7.3

Given below is the summarised production information for a manufacturing organisation for the last month:

Budgeted production in units	15,000
Actual production in units	14,200
Labour hours worked	46,000
Standard hours for each unit	3

(a) **Complete the table to calculate the following performance indicators and briefly explain what each one means give your answers to 2 dp):**

	Calculation	Explanation
Efficiency ratio		
Capacity ratio		
Production volume ratio		

(b) **If the workforce had operated at 95% efficiency how many labour hours would have been saved last month? Give your answer to the nearest whole number.**

	hours

Task 7.4

A division of Fooddrink Ltd is developing a new supplement and a colleague has prepared forecast information based upon two scenarios. The forecast statements of profit or loss (income statements), statements of financial position and performance ratios for both scenarios are shown below:

- Scenario 1 is to set the price at £10 per unit with sales of 120,000 units each year.

- Scenario 2 is to set the price at £5 per unit with sales of 360,000 units each year.

Budgeted statement of profit or loss (income statement)

	Scenario 1 £000	Scenario 2 £000
Revenue	1,200	1,800
Cost of production		
Direct (raw) materials	300	900
Direct labour	120	360
Fixed production overheads	360	360
Total cost of sales	780	1,620
Gross profit	**420**	**180**
Selling and distribution costs	74	122
Administration costs	100	100
Operating profit	**246**	**(42)**

Budgeted statement of financial position

	Scenario 1 £000	Scenario 2 £000
Non-current assets		
Machinery	1,600	1,600
Current assets		
Inventory of raw materials	50	50
Receivables	150	150
Current liabilities		
Payables	75	75
Net current assets	**125**	**125**
Long-term loans	754	1,042
Net assets	**971**	**683**
Represented by:		
Share capital	725	725
Operating profit for the year	246	(42)
Share capital and reserves	**971**	**683**

	Scenario 1	Scenario 2
Performance ratios		
Gross profit margin	35.00%	10.00%
Operating profit margin	20.50%	−2.33% (0%)
Direct materials as a percentage of revenue	25.00%	50.00%
Direct materials cost per unit	£2.50	£2.50
Return on net assets	25.33%	−6.15% (0%)

Required

(a) **Draft a report for the finance director giving an explanation of why the following ratios have changed:**

    (i)   **Gross profit margin**
    (ii) **Operating profit margin**
    (iii) **Direct materials as a percentage of revenue**

To: Finance Director
Subject: Differences in key performance indicators
From: Accounting Technician
Date: 18 June 20X7

Gross profit margin

Operating profit margin

Direct materials

You have found that your colleague has made a few mistakes with the figures for Scenario 2. The impact on gross profit, operating profit and net assets for Scenario 2 is shown below.

- Recalculated gross profit = £540,000
- Recalculated operating profit = £318,000
- Recalculated net assets = £1,043,000

(b) Recalculate the following ratios. Give your answers to TWO decimal places:

    (i)   Gross profit margin
    (ii)   Operating profit margin
    (iii) Return on net assets

(c) Redraft your report for the finance director commenting on the ratios you recalculated in (b) above and recommend whether the price of the product should be set at £10 or £5.

To:	Financial Director
Subject:	Differences in key performance indicators
From:	Accounting Technician
Date:	18 June 20X7

Gross profit margin

Operating profit margin

Return on net assets

Recommendations

Task 7.5

Given below is a summary of a business's performance for the last six months:

	July £000	Aug £000	Sept £000	Oct £000	Nov £000	Dec £000
Sales	560	540	500	550	580	600
Cost of sales	370	356	330	374	400	415
Expenses	123	119	110	116	122	131
Interest payable	–	–	–	3	3	3
Shareholders' funds	440	445	458	468	480	490
Loan	–	–	–	50	50	50

(a) **For each month of the year complete the table to calculate the performance indicators. Give your answers to the nearest whole number (unless otherwise indicated):**

	July	Aug	Sept	Oct	Nov	Dec
Gross profit margin						
Operating profit margin						
% of expenses to sales						
Return on capital employed (give answers to ONE dp)						
Asset turnover (give answers to ONE dp)						

(b) **Comment on what the figures calculated in part (a) show about the performance of the business over the last six months.**

[blank answer box]

Task 7.6

A manufacturing business has three small divisions, North, South and Central. The figures for the last three months of 20X6 for each division are given below:

	North £	South £	Central £
Financial details			
Sales	870,000	560,000	640,000
Opening inventory	34,000	41,000	34,000
Closing inventory	32,000	29,000	38,000
Purchases	590,000	380,000	420,000
Expenses	121,000	106,000	138,000
Share capital and reserves	980,000	690,000	615,000
Payables	103,400	42,600	66,700
Receivables	100,100	107,300	87,600
Non-financial details			
Factory floor area	500 sq m	400 sq m	420 sq m
Factory employees	18	12	15
Hours worked	8,500	5,800	7,000
Units produced	17,000	10,200	12,300

(a) **Complete the table to calculate the performance indicators for each division. Give your answer to ONE dp:**

	North	South	Central
Gross profit margin			
Operating profit margin			
Return on capital employed			
Asset turnover			
Inventory holding in months (using average inventory)			
Receivables' collection period in months			
Payables' collection period in months			
Units produced per square metre of floor area			
Units produced per employee			
Units produced per hour			

(b) **Use the performance indicators calculated in (a) to compare the performances of the three divisions for the three-month period.**

Task 7.7

(a) A business operates on a gross profit margin of 48% and sales for the period were £380,000.

The gross profit is £ [   ] .

(b) A business operates on a gross profit margin of 34% and the gross profit made in the period was £425,000.

The sales for the period were £ [   ] .

(c) A business had sales of £85,000 in a month and with a gross profit margin of 40% and an operating profit margin of 11.5%.

The expenses for the month were £ [   ] .

(d) A business has a return on capital employed of 11.6% and made an operating profit for the period of £100,000.

The capital employed is £ [   ] .

(e) A business has a net profit percentage of 8% and a return on capital employed of 10%.

The asset turnover of the business is [   ] .

(f) A business has opening inventory and closing inventory of £158,000 and £182,000 and made purchases during the year totalling £560,000.

Inventory turned over [   ] **times during the year.**

(g) A business has a receivables' collection period of 48 days and the closing receivables figure is £96,000.

The sales for the year are £ [   ] .

Task 7.8

Given below are the summarised statements of profit or loss (income statements) and statements of financial position of a business for the last two years.

Summarised statements of profit or loss (income statements)

	Y/e 31 Dec 20X8 £000	Y/e 31 Dec 20X7 £000
Revenue	602	564
Cost of sales	329	325
Gross profit	273	239
Expenses	163	143
Operating profit	110	96
Interest payable	10	10
Profit before tax	100	86

Summarised statements of financial position

| | 31 Dec 20X8 | | 31 Dec 20X7 | |
	£	£	£	£
Non-current assets		709		632
Current assets				
Inventory	28		32	
Receivables	66		68	
Cash	2		3	
	96		103	
Payables	55		45	
Net current assets		41		58
		750		690
Long term loan		150		150
		600		540
Share capital		300		300
Retained earnings		300		240
		600		540

(a) Complete the table for each of the two years to calculate the performance indicators, based on total capital employed when relevant.

	31 Dec 20X8	31 Dec 20X7
Gross profit margin (1 dp)		
Operating profit margin (1 dp)		
Return on capital employed (1 dp)		
Asset turnover (2 dp)		
Non-current asset turnover (2 dp)		
Current ratio (2 dp)		
Quick ratio (1 dp)		
Receivables' collection period (nearest day)		
Inventory holding in days (nearest day)		
Payables' payment period (nearest day)		
Interest cover (1 dp)		
Gearing ratio (1 dp)		

(b) Comment upon the performance of the business for the last two years basing your comments on the performance indicators calculated in part (a).

Task 7.9

Middle plc owns two subsidiaries, East Ltd and West Ltd, producing soft drinks. Both companies rent their premises and both use plants of similar size and technology. Middle plc requires the plant in the subsidiaries to be written off over ten years using straight-line depreciation and assuming zero residual values.

East Ltd was established five years ago but West Ltd has only been established for two years. Goods returned by customers generally arise from quality failures and are destroyed. Financial and other data relating to the two companies are reproduced below.

Statements of profit or loss (Income statements) year to 30 November 20X8			Statements of financial position extracts at 30 November 20X8		
	West Ltd £000	East Ltd £000		West Ltd £000	East Ltd £000
Revenue	18,000	17,600	Plant	16,000	10,000
Less Returns	90	176	Depreciation to date	3,200	5,000
Net revenue	17,910	17,424	Non-current assets	12,800	5,000
Material	2,000	2,640	Current assets	4,860	3,000
Labour	4,000	4,840	Current liabilities	(2,320)	(1,500)
Production overheads (Note)	3,000	3,080	Net assets	15,340	6,500
Gross profit	8,910	6,864			
Marketing	2,342	1,454			
Research & development	1,650	1,010			
Training	950	450			
Administration	900	1,155			
Operating profit	3,068	2,795			

Note. Includes plant depreciation of £1,600,000 for West Ltd and £1,000,000 for East Ltd

Other data (000's litres)	West Ltd	East Ltd			
Gross sales	20,000	22,000			
Returns	100	220			
Net sales	19,900	21,780			
Orders received in year	20,173	22,854			

You are employed by Middle plc as a member of a team monitoring the performance of subsidiaries within the group. Middle plc aims to provide its shareholders with the best possible return for their investment and to meet customers' expectations. It does this by comparing the performance of subsidiaries and using the more efficient ones for benchmarking.

Your team leader, Angela Wade, has asked you to prepare a report evaluating the performance of West Ltd and East Ltd. Your report should do the following:

Required

(a) **Calculate and explain the meaning of the following financial ratios for each company.**

    (i)   **The return on net assets (nearest whole percentage)**
    (ii)   **The net asset turnover (2 dp)**
    (iii) **The operating profit margin (1 dp)**

(b) **Calculate the percentage of faulty sales as a measure of the level of customer service for each company (to 1 dp).**

(c) **Identify ONE other possible measure of the level of customer service which could be derived from the accounting data.**

(d) **Identify TWO limitations to your analysis in task (a), using the data in the accounts.**

(a) **To:** Angela Wade
    From: A Technician
    Date: xx.xx.xx
    Subject: West Ltd and East Ltd – Performance Report

    (i)   Return on net assets (RONA)

(ii)   Net asset turnover

(iii)   Operating profit margin

(b)   Measure of customer service: faulty sales

(c)   Further measure of customer service

(d)   Limitations of financial ratios

Task 7.10

You are employed by Micro Circuits Ltd as a financial analyst reporting to Angela Frear, the Director of Corporate Strategy. One of your responsibilities is to monitor the performance of subsidiaries within the group. Financial and other data relating to subsidiary A is reproduced below.

Subsidiary A

Statement of profit or loss (Income statement) year to 30 November 20X8

	£000	£000
Revenue		4,000
Less returns		100
Net revenue (Note 1)		3,900
Material	230	
Labour	400	
Production overheads (Note 2)	300	
Cost of production	930	
Opening finished inventory	50	
Closing finished inventory	(140)	
Cost of sales		840
Gross profit		3,060
Marketing	500	
Customer support	400	
Research and development	750	
Training	140	
Administration	295	2,085
Operating profit		975

Extract from statement of financial position at 30 November 20X8

	£000	£000	£000
Non-current assets	Land and building	Plant and machinery	Total
Cost	2,000	2,500	4,500
Additions	–	1,800	1,800
	2,000	4,300	6,300
Accumulated dep'n	160	1,700	1,860
	1,840	2,600	4,440
Raw material inventory	15		
Finished goods inventory	140		
	155		
Receivables	325		
Cash and bank	40		
Payables	(85)		
			435
Net assets			4,875

Notes

1   **Analysis of revenue**

	£000		£000
Regular customers	3,120	New products	1,560
New customers	780	Existing products	2,340
	3,900		3,900

2   Production overheads include £37,200 of reworked faulty production.

3   Orders received in the year totalled £4,550,000.

Required

(a)   Angela Frear asks you to calculate the following performance indicators in preparation for a board meeting:

Performance indicator	Workings	
Return on net assets (nearest whole percentage)		
Net asset turnover (1 dp)		
Operating profit margin (nearest whole percentage)		
Average age of receivables in months (to nearest whole month)		
Average age of finished inventory in months (1 dp)		

One of the issues to be discussed at the board meeting is the usefulness of performance indicators. Angela Frear has recently attended a conference on creating and enhancing value.

Three criticisms were made of financial performance indicators:

•   They could give misleading signals.

•   They could be manipulated.

•   They focus on the short term and do not take account of other key, non-financial performance indicators.

At the conference, Angela was introduced to the idea of the balanced scorecard. The balanced scorecard looks at performance measurement from four perspectives:

The financial perspective

This is concerned with satisfying shareholders. Examples include the return on net assets and operating profit margin.

The customer perspective

This asks how customers view the business and is concerned with measures of customer satisfaction. Examples include speed of delivery and customer loyalty.

The internal perspective

This looks at the quality of the company's output in terms of technical excellence and customer needs. Examples would be striving towards total quality management and flexible production as well as unit cost.

The innovation and learning perspective

This is concerned with the continual improvement of existing products and the ability to develop new products as customers' needs change. An example would be the percentage of revenue attributable to new products.

(b) **Angela Frear asks you to prepare briefing notes for the board meeting. Using the data from part (a) where necessary, your notes should do the following:**

    (i)   **Suggest ONE reason why the return on net assets calculated in (a) might be misleading.**

    (ii)   **Identify ONE way of manipulating the operating profit margin.**

    (iii)   **Calculate the average delay in fulfilling orders.**

    (iv)   **Identify ONE other possible measure of customer satisfaction other than the delay in fulfilling orders.**

    (v)   **Calculate TWO indicators which may help to measure performance from an internal perspective.**

    (vi)   **Calculate ONE performance indicator which would help to measure the innovation and learning perspective.**

Briefing notes on the usefulness of performance indicators

Prepared for: Angela Frear

Prepared by: Financial Analyst

Dated: xx.xx.xx

(i)   Return on net assets

(ii)   Operating profit margin

(iii)   Average delay in fulfilling orders

(iv)   Measures of customer satisfaction

(v)   Measuring performance from an internal perspective

(vi)   Measuring the innovation and learning perspective

Task 7.11

Travel Bus Ltd is owned by Travel Holdings plc. It operates in the town of Camford. Camford is an old town with few parking facilities for motorists. Several years ago, the Town Council built a car park on the edge of the town and awarded Travel Bus the contract to carry motorists and their passengers between the car park and the centre of the town.

Originally, the Council charged motorists £4.00 per day for the use of the car park but, to encourage motorists not to take their cars into the town centre, parking has been free since 1 December 20X7.

The journey between the car park and the town centre is the only service operated by Travel Bus Ltd in Camford. A summary of the results for the first two years of operations, together with the net assets associated with the route and other operating data, is reproduced below.

Statement of profit or loss (Income statement) year ended 30 November			Extract from statement of financial position at 30 November		
	20X7 £	20X8 £		20X7 £	20X8 £
Revenue	432,000	633,600	Buses	240,000	240,000
Fuel	129,600	185,328	Accumulated depreciation	168,000	180,000
Wages	112,000	142,000	Non-current assets	72,000	60,000
Other variable costs	86,720	84,512	Net current assets	14,400	35,040
Gross profit	103,680	221,760		86,400	95,040
Bus road tax and insurance	22,000	24,000			
Depreciation of buses	12,000	12,000			
Maintenance of buses	32,400	28,512			
Fixed garaging costs	29,840	32,140			
Administration	42,000	49,076			
Operating profit/(loss)	(34,560)	76,032			

Other operating data	20X7	20X8
Fare per passenger journey	£0.80	£1.00
Miles per year	324,000	356,400
Miles per journey	18.0	18.0
Days per year	360	360
Wages per driver	£14,000	£14,200

Throughout the two years, the drivers were paid a basic wage per week, no bonuses were paid and no overtime was incurred.

In two weeks there will be a meeting between officials of the Town Council and the chief executive of Travel Holdings to discuss the performance of Travel Bus for the year to 30 November 20X8. The previous year's performance indicators were as follows.

Gross profit margin	24%
Operating profit margin	–8%
Return on capital employed	–40%
Asset turnover	5 times
Number of passengers in the year	540,000
Total cost per mile	£1.44
Number of journeys per day	50
Maintenance cost per mile	£0.10
Passengers per day	1,500
Passengers per journey	30
Number of drivers	8

Required

(a) **In preparation for the meeting, you have been asked to calculate the following performance indicators for the year to 30 November 20X8. Give your answers to the nearest whole number unless otherwise indicated.**

	Performance indicator for year to 30 November 20X8
(i) Gross profit margin	
(ii) Operating profit margin	
(iii) Return on capital employed	
(iv) Asset turnover (to the nearest dp)	

	Performance indicator for year to 30 November 20X8
(v) Number of passengers in the year	
(vi) Total cost per mile (to the nearest two dps)	
(vii) Number of journeys per day	
(viii) Maintenance cost per mile (to the nearest two dps)	
(ix) Passengers per day	
(x) Passengers per journey	
(xi) Number of drivers	

On receiving your performance indicators, the chief executive of Travel Holdings raises the following issues with you:

- The drivers are claiming that the improved profitability of Travel Bus reflects their increased productivity.

- The managers believe that the change in performance is due to improved motivation arising from the introduction of performance related pay for managers during the year to 30 November 20X8.

- The officials from the Town Council are concerned that Travel Bus is paying insufficient attention to satisfying passenger needs and safety.

The chief executive asks for your advice.

(b) Write a memo to the chief executive of Travel Holdings plc. Where relevant, you should make use of the data and answers to task a) to do the following:

(i) Briefly discuss whether or not increased productivity always leads to increased profitability.

(ii) Develop ONE possible measure of driver productivity and suggest whether or not the drivers' claim is valid.

(iii) Suggest ONE reason, other than improved motivation, why the profitability of Travel Bus might have improved.

(iv) (1) Suggest ONE existing performance indicator which might measure the satisfaction of passenger needs.

(2) Suggest ONE other possible performance indicator of passenger needs which cannot be measured from the existing performance data collected by Travel Bus.

(v) (1) **Suggest ONE existing performance indicator which might measure the safety aspect of Travel Bus's operations.**

     (2) **Suggest ONE other possible performance indicator which cannot be measured from the existing performance data collected by Travel Bus.**

MEMO

To: Chief executive
From: Management accountant
Date: xx.xx.xx
Subject: Performance of Travel Bus Ltd for the year to 30 November 20X8

This memo addresses a number of issues concerning the productivity and profitability of Travel Bus Ltd.

(i)   Productivity and profitability

(ii)   Driver productivity

(iii) Reason for improved profitability

(iv)   Performance indicators to measure the satisfaction of passenger needs

(v)   Monitoring the safety aspect of Travel Bus's operations

---

Task 7.12

TeesRus Ltd makes and packs tea bags. The company currently has eight Pickmaster machines, which are coming to the end of their useful life. The company is considering replacing all eight machines with either new Pickmaster machines or new Pickmaster 2 machines.

Each new Pickmaster machine costs £20,000 and requires 10 operators per day for the 100 days of the harvest. The machine will have a life of 10 years and a depreciation charge of £2,000 per year.

A new Pickmaster 2 machine requires only one operator per day for the 100 days. This machine costs £90,000 to purchase and will have a life of 10 years. The depreciation charge will be £9,000 per year.

Other budgeted information for 20X8 is as follows:

- The forecast harvest will last 100 days and produce 2.5 million kilograms of tea.

- The selling price of tea will be 45 pence per kilogram.

- Budgeted revenue is £1,125,000.

- Tea picker costs will be £150,000.

- Tea processor operators currently earn £6 per day.

- The tea pickers and tea processor operators are employed as and when needed on temporary contracts.

- Seed and fertiliser costs will be £75,000.

- Administration costs will be £150,000 if the Pickmaster machines are purchased.

- Administration costs will be £135,000 if the Pickmaster 2 machines are purchased.

- Distribution costs will be £350,000.

- The net assets at the end of the period will be £935,500 plus the budgeted operating profit.

- Disposing of the old machines will incur no profit, loss or any depreciation charge during 20X8.

Required

(a) Prepare TWO budgeted statements of profit or loss (income statements) and net asset workings assuming that the business purchases either eight Pickmaster or eight Pickmaster 2 machines.

Budgeted statements of profit or loss (income statements)

	Pickmaster £	Pickmaster 2 £
Revenue		
Cost of sales		
Tea pickers		
Tea processor operators		
Depreciation		
Seed and fertiliser costs		
Total cost of sales		
Gross profit		
Administration costs		
Distribution costs		
Operating profit		

Net assets at year end

	Pickmaster £	Pickmaster 2 £
Budgeted net assets		
Operating profit		

(b) **Complete the table to calculate the following indicators for each option (to 2 dp):**

	Pickmaster	Pickmaster 2
Gross profit margin		
Operating profit margin		
Return on net assets		

(c) **Prepare a report for the managing director to include the following:**

(i) **Comments on the indicators calculated in part (b) above.**

(ii) **Two other considerations.**

(iii) **A recommendation whether to purchase the Pickmaster or Pickmaster 2 machines.**

REPORT

To: Managing Director
From: Accounting technician
Date: December 20X7
Subject: Purchase of new machinery

Performance indicators

Other considerations

Conclusion

Task 7.13

BeThere Airlines is reviewing its catering division and has provided the following information for the previous three months. The division has no administration or distribution costs. All costs are treated as costs of sales. All production has to be used in that day.

Catering Division

Cost report for the three-month period	September £	October £	November £
Revenue	690,000	697,200	672,000
Cost of production			
Direct materials	185,000	185,100	185,220
Direct labour	274,313	275,975	279,300
Fixed production overheads	82,000	82,000	82,000
Total cost of sales	541,313	543,075	546,520
Profit	148,687	154,125	125,480
Catering Division statement of financial position	September £	October £	November £
Non-current assets			
Land and buildings	800,000	795,000	790,000
Machinery	480,000	460,000	420,000
Current assets			
Inventory of raw materials	231,000	251,500	307,800
Amounts due from Airlines Division	690,000	697,200	672,000
Current liabilities			
Trade payables	190,000	185,000	185,100
Net current assets	731,000	763,700	794,700
Non-current liabilities	800,000	800,000	800,000
Net assets	1,211,000	1,218,700	1,204,700
	Units	Units	Units
Capacity (meals per month)	125,000	125,000	125,000
Meals ordered by Flights Division	115,000	117,000	112,000
Budgeted meals	115,000	117,000	112,000
Meals produced	115,500	116,200	117,600

Required

(a) Calculate the following performance indicators for each month, expressing each answer to two decimal places:

(i) Profit margin
(ii) Direct material cost as a percentage of revenue
(iii) Direct labour cost as a percentage of revenue
(iv) Return on capital employed (ROCE)
(v) Meals produced as a percentage of orders
(vi) Meals produced as a percentage of capacity

(b) Draft a brief report to the managing director commenting on the performance of the division in November. You should base your report on your calculations above.

REPORT

To: Managing Director
From: Accounting Technician
Subject: Performance of the Catering Division
Date: 7 December 20X6

The operations director is now reviewing various alternatives to determine whether it is possible to reduce monthly costs.

She is considering whether to invest in a new machine which:

- Will mechanise part of the process and reduce the labour cost per meal from the current rate of £2.375 to £1.50

- Could either be purchased for £3 million or rented for £50,000 per month

- Is expected to have a life of 10 years and a scrap value of £900,000

If the company purchases the machine, the division's net assets as at the end of November will increase by £1 million plus the profit for the period.

If the company rents the machine, the division's net assets will only increase by the profit for the period.

The operations director's performance is measured on ROCE, which she would like to see improved.

Required

(c) (i) **Prepare a forecast statement of profit or loss (income statement) and net asset calculation (a full statement of financial position is not required) for both options (renting and purchasing) for one month.**

   Note. Assume that the number of meals produced and sold will be 120,000 per month at a cost of £6 per meal. The material cost will remain as standard at £2 per meal, and monthly overheads will stay at £82,000 before any additional costs of the new machine. Ignore the time value of money.

(ii) **Calculate the profit margin and the ROCE for both options (to 2 dp).**

(iii) **What action would you recommend to the operations director?**

Task 7.14

A company makes two products, S1 and S2. The following information is available for the year:

	S1	S2
Sales volume (units)	50,000	100,000
	£	£
Sales price per unit	20	16
Total sales revenue	1,000,000	1,600,000
Material costs	300,000	600,000
Labour costs	300,000	600,000
Fixed production costs	250,000	250,000
Total cost of sales	850,000	1,450,000
Gross profit	150,000	150,000
Material cost per unit	£6.00	£6.00
Labour cost per unit	£6.00	£6.00
Fixed production cost per unit	£5.00	£2.50
Gross profit margin	15.00%	9.38%

Explain why the gross profit margin is different between S1 and S2 by considering the following:

(a)   **Sales price and sales volume**
(b)   **Material cost**
(c)   **Fixed production cost**

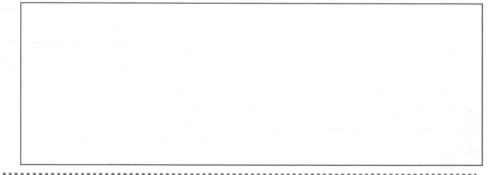

Task 7.15

You have been provided with the following information for two scenarios involving a company which operates an absorption costing system:

	Scenario 1	Scenario 2
Sales volume (units)	120,000	150,000
	£	£
Revenue	1,680,000	1,800,000
Gross profit	600,000	450,000
Profit from operations	275,000	200,000
Net assets	2,298,400	2,100,340
Inventory	147,950	167,500

(a) **Calculate the following performance indicators for Scenario 1 and 2. Give your answers to TWO dp.**

	Scenario 1	Scenario 2
Return on net assets		
Inventory holding period in days		
Sales price per unit		
Full production cost per unit		

(b) **Complete the table below for Scenario 3.**

	Scenario 3
Net assets (£)	175,000
Return on net assets (%)	13
Profit margin (%)	14
Gearing (%)	32.75
Profit (to the nearest £)	
Sales revenue (to the nearest £)	

(c) **Fill in the boxes with the appropriate options to show how to calculate the gearing. If there is more than one correct answer either answer will achieve full marks.**

$$\frac{\boxed{}}{\boxed{}} \times \boxed{}$$

Options:

Total Debt	Profit	365
Net Assets	Total Equity	100
Total Debt plus Total Equity	Total Debt less Total Equity	%

Task 7.16

The following information, shown in the statement of profit or loss below, has been supplied for two different companies. The sales volume of Company A is 900,000 units and for Company B is 1,400,000 units.

Statement of profit or loss

	Company A £000	Company B £000
Total sales revenue	37,800	49,000
Production costs		
Material cost	6,300	8,400
Labour cost	16,200	16,800
Fixed production cost	3,150	4,200
Total cost of sales	25,650	29,400
Gross profit	**12,150**	**19,600**
Selling and distribution costs	900	1,680
Administration costs	1,980	2,940
Advertising costs	1,260	3,220
Profit	**8,010**	**11,760**
Additional information		
Net assets	89,000	60,000

(a) **Complete the table below by calculating the performance indicators for Company A and Company B. If rounding is required, show your answer to two dp.**

	Company A	Company B
Selling price per unit (£)		
Labour cost per unit (£)		
Fixed production cost per unit (£)		
Selling and distribution costs as (a % of revenue)		
Gross profit margin (%)		
Profit margin (%)		
Return on net assets (%)		

You have been requested to calculate control ratios for a company. The following has been provided to assist you in making the calculations:

Labour efficiency ratio

Standard hours for actual production/actual hours worked expressed as a percentage

Capacity ratio

Actual hours worked/Budgeted hours expressed as a percentage

Activity ratio

Actual output/Budgeted output expressed as a percentage

Data is available for two years:

	Year 1	Year 2
Budgeted production (units)	42,000	48,000
Standard hours per unit	0.8 hours	0.8 hours
Actual hours worked	30,920 hours	38,720 hours
Actual production (units)	37,200	51,000

(b)   Calculate the labour efficiency ratio for each year. Round your answers to two dp.

Ratio	Year 1 %	Year 2 %
Labour efficiency ratio		

Task 7.17

Given below are production and sales figures for a manufacturing organisation for the last three months:

	January	February	March
Production costs	£552,300	£568,500	£629,500
Production wages	£104,800	£98,300	£110,800
Output in units	8,540	8,670	9,320
Hours worked	8,635	7,820	9,280
Budgeted output	8,500	8,200	9,500
Sales revenue	£916,000	£923,000	£965,000
Number of employees	55	55	58

Production costs are made up of the materials for production and the bought in services required in the month. It is estimated that each unit takes 1.1 hours to produce.

Required

Complete the table to calculate the performance indicators for each of the last three months. Give your answers to the TWO decimal places:

	January	February	March
Productivity per labour hour			
Efficiency ratio			
Capacity ratio			
Activity ratio			
Value added per employee			

....

Task 7.18

A company makes and sells a single product. The forecast statement of profit or loss (income statement) and statement of financial position are shown below.

The forecast is based on an assumed sales price of £8 per unit, and anticipated demand of 500,000 units.

Budgeted statement of profit or loss (income statement)

	£000
Revenue	4,000
Cost of production	
Direct materials	1,500
Direct labour	500
Fixed production overheads	800
Total cost of sales	2,800
Gross profit	**1,200**
Fixed selling and distribution costs	85
Fixed administration costs	210
Operating profit	**905**

Budgeted statement of financial position

	£000
Non-current assets	
Machinery	1,600
Current assets	
Inventory of raw materials	280
Receivables	800
Current liabilities	
Payables	(150)
Net current assets	**930**
Long-term loans	500
Net assets	**2,030**
Represented by:	
Share capital and reserves	2,030
Net assets	**2,030**

Required

Draft a report to the finance director:

(a) Include calculations of the performance indicators listed below. Give your answers to the nearest whole number.

    (i)   **Gross profit margin**

    (ii)   **Operating profit margin**

    (iii) **Direct materials cost per unit**

    (iv) **Receivables' collection period in days**

(b) Advises on the following scenarios:

    (i)   The gross profit margin for the industry is 35%. Advise the finance director, what the selling price would have to be if demand and costs stay the same, in order to achieve this margin.

    (ii)   The operating profit margin for the industry is 25%. If it is not possible to change the selling price, demand or most costs, but it may be possible to reduce fixed administration costs, what would the percentage reduction in fixed administration costs have to be, in order to achieve a gross profit margin of 25%?

    (iii) The average receivables' payment period in the industry is 65 days. If sales are unchanged, advise the finance director by how much (in £) the year-end receivables would have to change, to achieve the industry average payment period.

To:	Finance Director
Subject:	Key performance indicators
From:	Accounting Technician
Date:	26 October 20X2

Gross profit margin – selling price to achieve industry margin

Operating profit margin – percentage reduction in administration costs

Receivables' collection period – change to achieve industry average

Appendix

	£
Gross profit margin	
Operating profit margin	
Direct materials cost per unit	
Receivables' collection period in days	

Chapter 8 – Cost management

Task 8.1

(a) **Explain the five stages of the product lifecycle and how costs and income will alter in each of the five stages.**

(b) **Explain how knowledge of the product lifecycle affects forecasting of future sales?**

Task 8.2

A company is developing a new product. There are currently several other companies manufacturing similar products which sell for a price of £50 each. The company wishes to make a margin of 20%.

The target cost of the new product is £ _____ .

Task 8.3

A company can sell 10,000 units in the next year, giving total sales of £250,000. The company wants to make a profit margin of 70%.

The target cost per unit is £ [   ] .

Task 8.4

Alpha Limited is considering designing a new product, product BPT, and will use target costing to arrive at the target cost of the product.

You have been given the following information:

- The price at which the product will be sold has not yet been decided.

- It has been estimated that if the price is set at £40 the demand will be 500,000 units, and if the price is set at £50 the demand will be 430,000 units.

- The costs of production include fixed production costs of £8,500,000 which will give a production capacity of 500,000 units.

- In order to produce above this level the fixed costs will step up by £1,500,000.

- The required profit margin is 30%.

- The variable cost per unit is £13 for the production volume of 430,000 units.

- For production volume of 500,000 units the variable cost will be £12 per unit.

(a) **Complete the table for both levels of demand.**

	Sales price £40	Sales price £50
The target total production cost per unit		
The target fixed production cost per unit		
The target fixed production cost		

(b) **Complete the following sentence:**

Alpha should set the price at [▼] in order to achieve the target profit margin.

Picklist:

£40
£50

....

Task 8.5

A company manufactures and sells an electronic product and is preparing information for the next period.

The marketing department has estimated that if the price is set at £70 the demand will be 10,000 units and if the price is set at £90 the demand will be 6,000 units.

The cost information below has been provided by the finance department.

	Option 1	Option 2
Sales price	£70	£90
Sales volume	10,000	6,000
Costs	**£**	**£**
Variable materials cost	20	20
Variable labour cost	10	10
Fixed production cost per unit	24	40
Total cost	54	70

The production manager says that the capacity of the factory is 8,000 units.

(a) **Calculate the profit achieved if the price is set at £90 and the demand is 6,000 units.**

The profit achieved is [£   ] .

(b) **Calculate the profit achieved if the price is set at £70 and the demand is 10,000 units but the factory can only produce 8,000 units.**

The profit achieved is [£   ] .

An overseas supplier has offered to manufacture 4,000 units at a price of £45.

(c) **Calculate the profit achieved if the price is set at £70 with demand of 10,000 units, manufacturing 6,000 units and purchasing 4,000 units from the overseas supplier.**

The profit achieved is £ [   ] .

Company Alpha is developing a new product and expects the target cost to be £50 and will set the sales price to achieve a profit margin of 20%.

(d) **Complete the following sentence:**

The sales price per unit will need to be £ [   ] to achieve

a profit margin of 20%.

Company Beta sells a product with a mark up of 30% on cost. The cost of the product is £80.

(e) **Complete the following sentence:**

The sales price to achieve a mark up of 30% is

£ [   ] .

BPP
LEARNING MEDIA

Chapter 9 – Activity based costing (ABC)

Task 9.1

Charleroi Aircon Ltd design and install industrial air-conditioning systems. The company is based in Birmingham.

Charleroi's usual pricing policy is to use direct costs (equipment and installation labour) plus a mark-up of 50% to establish the selling price for an air-conditioning installation.

The company is about to tender for two contracts, quotation HMG/012 and quotation CFG/013.

The company is in the process of designing an activity based costing (ABC) system and the following information has been obtained about the two jobs.

Estimates related to contracts HMG/012 and CFG/013			
Contract number:		HMG/012	CFG/013
Equipment:	Cost	£175,000	£120,000
	Number of items purchased	650	410
Direct labour:	Hours	10,000	6,000
	Hourly rate	£13	£11
Design hours		1,280	620
Distance from Birmingham office (miles round-trip)		320	90
Engineer site visits required		30	10

The following overhead information is also available in relation to ABC costs:

ABC details for overhead activities connected with air conditioning installation contracts			
Activity	Budgeted cost pool £pa	Cost driver	Cost driver units pa
Design department	675,000	Design hours	25,000
Site engineers	370,000	Miles travelled	185,000
Purchasing department	105,000	Items purchased	15,000
Payroll department	75,000	Direct hours	300,000
Site management	750,000	Direct hours	300,000
Post-installation inspection	80,000	Items purchased	20,000

(a) The price of job HMG/012 based upon direct costs plus 50% mark-up is

£ [ ] .

The price of job CFG/013 based upon direct costs plus 50% mark-up is

£ [ ] .

(b) Complete the tables to show the activity based overhead costs for each of jobs HMG/012 and CFG/013.

Activity	Budgeted cost pool £	Cost driver	Cost driver units pa	Cost per unit of cost driver £
Design department				
Site engineers				
Purchasing department				
Payroll dept				
Site management				
Post-installation inspection				

Cost pool	Total cost HMG/012 £	Total cost CFG/013 £
Design department		
Site engineers		
Purchasing department		
Payroll dept		
Site management		
Post-installation inspection		
Total cost		

Task 9.2

You are employed as a financial analyst at Drampton plc, a computer retailer. Drampton plc has recently taken over Little Ltd, a small company making personal computers and servers. Little appears to make all of its profits from servers. Drampton's finance director tells you that Little's fixed overheads are currently charged to production using standard labour hours and gives you their standard cost of making PCs and servers. These are shown below.

Little Ltd: Standard cost per computer

Model	Server	PC
Annual budgeted volume	5	5,000
Unit standard cost	**£**	**£**
Material and labour	50,000	500
Fixed overhead	4,000	40
Standard cost per unit	54,000	540

The finance director asks for your help and suggests you reclassify the fixed overheads between the two models using activity based costing. You are given the following information:

(a)   Budgeted total annual fixed overheads

	£
Set-up costs	10,000
Rent and power (production area)	120,000
Rent (stores area)	50,000
Salaries of store issue staff	40,000
Total	220,000

Every time Little makes a server, it has to stop making PCs and rearrange the factory layout. The cost of this is shown as set-up costs. If the factory did not make any servers these costs would be eliminated.

(b) Cost drivers

	Server	PC	Total
Number of set-ups	5	0	5
Number of weeks of production	10	40	50
Floor area of stores (square metres)	400	400	800
Number of issues of inventory	2,000	8,000	10,000

Required

Complete the table to show how to reallocate Little's budgeted total fixed annual overheads between server and PC production on an ABC basis.

	Server allocated overheads £	PC allocated overheads £
Set-up costs		
Rent and power (production area)		
Rent (stores area)		
Salaries of stores issue staff		
Total overheads		

Task 9.3

You are the management accountant at a manufacturing company which makes two products, the Plastic and the Metal. Standard costing information for direct material and labour costs are given for the two products below.

Product	Plastic	Metal
Budgeted production units	5,000	1,000
Unit standard cost	**£**	**£**
Material	10	25
Labour	2	4

The company has the following budgeted overheads:

	£
Power for machinery	110,000
Rent of factory	120,000
Canteen costs	40,000
Total	270,000

The cost drivers for these costs are given below, for the different products:

Cost drivers

	Plastic	Metal	Total
Machine hours	2,500	3,000	5,500
Floor space (square metres)	1,000	200	1,200
Number of employees	200	50	250

Required

Complete the table to show how to reallocate the budgeted total overheads between the two products on an ABC basis.

	Plastic allocated overheads £	Metal allocated overheads £
Power for machinery		
Rent of factory		
Canteen costs		
Total overheads		

Chapter 10 – Decision making techniques

Task 10.1

A business sells a single product and has budgeted sales of 115,000 units for the next period. The selling price per unit is £28 and the variable costs of production are £17. The fixed costs of the business are £1,100,000.

The breakeven point in units is ⬚ units.

The margin of safety in units is ⬚ units.

The margin of safety as a percentage of budgeted sales is ⬚ %.

....

Task 10.2

The following information relates to one period for Product D which is manufactured by Mild Ltd.

Expected sales revenue = £160,000
Selling price per unit = £16 per unit
Variable cost = £8 per unit
Fixed costs = £40,000

The breakeven point both in terms of units and sales revenue is:

Units	✓
5,000	
10,000	

Sales revenue £	✓
40,000	
80,000	

....

Task 10.3

The following information relates to one period for Product V which is manufactured by Hay-on-Wye Ltd.

Selling price per unit = £80
Variable cost per unit = £25
Budgeted fixed costs = £110,000
Budgeted sales = 2,500 units

The margin of safety, in terms of both units and sales revenue is:

Units	✓
500	
2,000	
1,900	
500	

Sales revenue £	✓
12,500	
160,000	
152,000	
40,000	

Task 10.4

A business sells a single product at a selling price of £83 and the variable costs of production and sales are £65 per unit. The fixed costs of the business are £540,000.

The number of units of the product that the business must sell in order to make a target profit of £300,000 is _____ **units.**

Task 10.5

A business sells its single product for £40. The variable costs of this product total £28. The fixed costs of the business are £518,000.

The sales revenue required in order to make a target profit of £250,000 is £ [   ] .

....

Task 10.6

Three products are produced by a business. There is a shortage of the material which is used to make each product, with only 3,000 kg available in the coming period.

	Product		
	A	B	C
Direct materials @ £4 per kg	£8	£4	£16
Direct labour @ £10 per hour	£20	£5	£15
Selling price	£40	£25	£47
Maximum sales demand	1,000 units	800 units	600 units

Complete the table to determine the production plan which will maximise contribution.

Product	Units

....

Task 10.7

A business produces three products. Production and sales details are given below:

	Product		
	R	S	T
Direct materials @ £5 per kg	£20	£25	£15
Direct labour @ £7 per hour	£14	£21	£21
Selling price	£45	£60	£55
Machine hours per unit	4	3	2
Maximum sales demand	20,000 units	25,000 units	8,000 units

During the next period the supply of materials is limited to 250,000 kgs, the labour hours available are 100,000 and the machine hours available are 180,000.

Complete the table to determine the production plan which will maximise contribution.

Product	Units

The contribution that will be earned under this production plan is

£ _____ .

Task 10.8

An organisation makes two products, X and Y. The following information is available for the next month:

	Product X £ per unit	Product Y £ per unit
Selling prices	100	135
Variable costs		
Material cost (£5 per kilogram)	30	40
Labour cost	25	38
Total variable costs	55	78
Fixed costs		
Fixed production costs	12	15
Fixed administration costs	8	8
Total fixed costs	20	23
Profit per unit	25	34
Monthly demand	3,500	4,250

The materials are in short supply in the coming month and only 45,000 kilograms of material will be available.

(a)   Complete the following table, rounding to the nearest penny:

	Product X £	Product Y £
The contribution per unit is		
The contribution per kilogram of materials		

(b)   The optimal production order for products X, and Y is _____ ▼ .

Picklist:

product X then product Y
product Y then product X

(c)   **Complete the table below for the optimal production mix.**

	Product X Units	Product Y Units
Production		

(d)   **Complete the table below for the total contribution for each product.**

	Product X £	Product Y £
Total contribution		

Task 10.9

Alpha makes two products, Tig and Tag. The following information is available for the next month:

	Product Tig £ per unit	Product Tag £ per unit
Selling price	4,000	4,950
Variable costs		
Material cost (£400 per kilogram)	2,400	3,000
Labour cost	400	600
Total variable cost	2,800	3,600
Fixed costs		
Production cost	450	450
Administration cost	300	300
Total fixed costs	750	750
Profit per unit	450	600
Monthly demand	200 units	300 units

The materials are in short supply in the coming month and only 3,000 kilograms of material will be available from the existing supplier.

(a) **Complete the table below.**

	Product Tig £	Product Tag £
The contribution per unit is		
The contribution per kilogram of materials is		

(b) **Complete the following statement:**

The optimal production order for products Tig and Tag is [▼] .

Picklist:

Tag then Tig
Tig then Tag

(c) **Complete the table below for the optimal production mix.**

	Product Tig Units	Product Tag Units
Production		

(d) **Complete the table below for the total contribution for each product.**

	Product Tig £	Product Tag £
Total contribution		

Alpha has been approached by another materials supplier who can supply up to 500 kilograms of material at a cost per kilogram of £500. This is a premium of £100 above the normal cost per kilogram.

(e) **Complete the table below.**

Should Alpha purchase the additional material?	Give a reason
[▼]	[▼]

Picklist:

No
Yes

Picklist:

The additional cost per kilogram is greater than the contribution per kilogram.
The additional cost per kilogram is greater than the contribution per unit.
The additional cost per kilogram is less than the contribution per kilogram.
The additional cost per kilogram is less than the contribution per unit.

Task 10.10

The following annual sales and cost information relating to labelled food containers types A and B were originally budgeted to be:

	Product	
	A	**B**
Units made and sold	300,000	500,000
Sales revenue (£)	450,000	600,000
Direct materials (£)	60,000	125,000
Direct labour (£)	36,000	70,000
Variable overheads (£)	45,000	95,000

Total fixed costs attributable to A and B are budgeted to be £264,020.

The £264,020 of fixed costs attributed to products A and B can be split between the two products: £158,620 to A and £105,400 to B.

After a difficult few months the annual sales were forecast and revised. The latest sales forecast is that 250,000 units of product A and 400,000 units of product B will be sold during the year.

(a) Complete the table below to calculate:

(i) The budgeted break-even sales, in units, for each of the two products

(ii) The margin of safety (in units) for each of the two products

(iii) The margin of safety as a percentage (to 2 dp)

	Product	
	A	B
Fixed costs (£)		
Unit contribution (£)		
Breakeven sales (units)		
Forecast sales (units)		
Margin of safety (units)		
Margin of safety (%) (2dp)		

(b) **Explain which of the two products, A or B, has the better margin of safety and why.**

Task 10.11

A business has calculated the margin of safety for its product for each of three levels of forecast sales as follows:

	Forecast sales (units)		
	1,000	1,200	1,500
Breakeven (units)	1,200	1,200	1,200
Margin of safety (units)	(200)	0	300
Margin of safety (%) (2dp)	–	0%	20%

Explain the significance of the percentage margin of safety for each of the three feasible activity levels.

Task 10.12

A company is considering the purchase of a small sole trader's business for a cost of £84,000 on 30 June 20X5. The estimated cash inflows from the purchased business are:

	£
30 June 20X6	26,000
30 June 20X7	30,000
30 June 20X8	21,000
30 June 20X9	14,000

Thereafter the purchased business will be closed down and its operations merged with the other operations of the company.

The company has a cost of capital of 7% and analyses potential investments using the net present value method.

The discount factors at 7% are as follows:

Year	Discount factor
0	1.000
1	0.935
2	0.873
3	0.816
4	0.763

The net present value of the investment is £ _____ .

Task 10.13

The managers of a business are considering investing in a new factory. It has been estimated that the cost now would total £355,000. The anticipated profit for the factory for each of the next five years are as follows:

	Profit £
Year 1	47,000
Year 2	55,000
Year 3	68,000
Year 4	53,000
Year 5	22,000

The profit figures given are after charging depreciation of £60,000 in each year. The business has a cost of capital of 12%.

The discount factors at 12% are as follows:

Year	Discount factor
0	1.000
1	0.893
2	0.797
3	0.712
4	0.635
5	0.567

The net present value of the potential investment is:

£

Task 10.14

Beta Limited will be replacing some machines in the next year and needs to decide whether to purchase or lease the machines.

(a) **Calculate the discounted lifecycle cost of purchasing the machines based upon the following:**

- **Purchase price of £400,000**
- **Annual running costs of £50,000 in Year 1 increasing by 5% for Year 2 and another 5% for Year 3 and then remaining constant for the next two years**
- **The running costs are paid annually in arrears**
- **A residual value of £35,000 at the end of the five years**

If there are nil cashflows for any years you MUST enter 0 in the appropriate box. Net cash outflows must be shown as positive figures and net cash inflows as negative figures (use minus signs).

Round to the nearest whole £.

	Year					
	0	1	2	3	4	5
Cash flow (£)						
Discounted factor	1	0.952	0.907	0.864	0.823	0.784
Present value (£)						
Net present cost (£)						

(b) Calculate the discounted lifecycle cost of leasing the machines for five years based upon annual costs of £140,000 paid annually in advance.

If there are nil cashflows for any years you MUST enter 0 in the appropriate box. Net cash outflows must be shown as positive figures and net cash inflows as negative figures (use brackets).

Round to the nearest whole £.

	Year					
	0	1	2	3	4	5
Cash flow (£)				(140,000)		
Discounted factor	1	0.952	0.907	0.864	0.823	0.784
Present value (£)						
Net present cost (£)						

(c) **Complete the following sentence:**

Based on the calculations it is best to [▼] as this saves

£ [ ] .

Picklist:

lease
purchase

Answer Bank

Chapter 1

Task 1.1

	✓
True	
False	✓

	16,000 units £	**22,000 units** £
Total cost	54,400	68,200
Cost per unit	3.40	3.10

Therefore, this is not a variable cost – if it were a true variable cost then the cost per unit would be the same at each activity level.

Task 1.2

Cost	Behaviour
Cost I	Variable
Cost II	Semi-variable or stepped
Cost III	Fixed
Cost IV	Variable

Workings

1   **Cost I**

£7,000/1,000 units = £7 per unit

£10,500/1,500 units = £7 per unit

Costs increase in direct proportion to output, therefore cost is variable.

2   **Cost II**

£11,000/1,000 units = £11 per unit

£12,50/1,500 units = £8.33 per unit

Costs increase but not in direct proportion to output, therefore cost is semi-variable or stepped.

3   **Cost III**

Cost remains the same regardless of level of output, therefore cost is fixed.

4   **Cost IV**

£3,800/1,000 units = £3.8 per unit

£5,700/1,500 units = £3.8 per unit

Costs increase in direct proportion to output, therefore cost is variable.

Task 1.3

Activity level Units	Total production cost £	Cost per unit £
8,000	50,600	6.325
12,000	63,400	5.283
15,000	73,000	4.867

Working:

	8,000 units £	12,000 units £	15,000 units £
Variable costs			
£32,000/10,000 × 8,000	25,600		
£32,000/10,000 × 12,000		38,400	
£32,000/10,000 × 15,000			48,000
Fixed costs	25,000	25,000	25,000
	50,600	63,400	73,000
Cost per unit	6.325	5.283	4.867

Task 1.4

Activity level Units	Total supervisors cost £	Supervisors cost per unit £
500	20,000	40.00
1,000	40,000	40.00
1,500	40,000	26.67

Working:

	500 units £	1,000 units £	1,500 units £
Number of supervisors required			
500/750 = 0.67, round up to 1 @ £20,000	20,000		
1,000/750 = 1.33, round up to 2 @ £20,000		40,000	
1,500/750 = 2 @ £20,000			40,000
Cost per unit	40	40	26.67

Task 1.5

	Cost behaviour
Maintenance department costs which are made up of £25,000 of salaries and an average of £500 cost per call out	Semi-variable
Machinery depreciation based upon machine hours used	Variable
Salary costs of nursery school teachers where one teacher is required for every six children in the nursery	Stepped fixed
Rent for a building that houses the factory, stores and maintenance departments	Fixed

Task 1.6

(a)

Production level Units	Total cost of production £	Cost per unit £
1,000	82,000	82.00
1,500	112,500	75.00
2,000	143,000	71.50

Working:

	1,000 units £	1,500 units £	2,000 units £
Direct materials 6kgs × £4.80 × units	28,800	43,200	57,600
Direct labour 4 hours × £7.00 × units	28,000	42,000	56,000
Building costs – fixed	18,000	18,000	18,000
Leased machines	1,200	1,800	2,400
Stores costs £3,000 + £3.00 × units	6,000	7,500	9,000
	82,000	112,500	143,000
Cost per unit	82.00	75.00	71.50

(b) The cost per unit is decreasing as production quantities increase. This is due to the fact that not all of the costs are variable. The buildings costs are fixed and part of the stores costs are also fixed. For these elements of total cost, as the production quantity increases, the cost per unit decreases. This in turn reduces the total overall unit cost as the quantity increases.

··

Task 1.7

The variable cost per machine hour is £ 15.00 .

The fixed costs of the maintenance department are £ £72,000 .

Workings

1 **Variable costs**

	Machine hours	Cost £
June (lowest)	14,200	285,000
August (highest)	15,200	300,000
Increase	1,000	15,000
Variable cost = £15,000/1,000 hours		
= £15 per hour		

2 **Fixed costs: June**

	Cost £
Variable element £15 × 14,200 hours	213,000
Fixed element (bal fig)	72,000
Total cost	285,000

· ·

Task 1.8

(a) The fixed element of the production cost is £ | 167,000 |.

The variable element of the production cost per unit is £ | 7 |.

Working:

	Activity level	Cost £
July (lowest)	63,000	608,000
September (highest)	76,000	699,000
Increase	13,000	91,000
Variable element = £91,000/13,000		
= £7 per unit		

	Activity level	Cost £
Fixed costs		
July		
Variable element £7 × 63,000 units		441,000
Fixed element (bal fig)		167,000
Total cost		608,000

(b)

Level of production Units	Production cost £
74,000	685,000
90,000	797,000

Workings

1 **Production level of 74,000 units**

	£
Variable cost £7 × 74,000	518,000
Fixed cost	167,000
Total cost	685,000

2 **Production level of 90,000 units**

	£
Variable cost £7 × 90,000	630,000
Fixed cost	167,000
Total cost	797,000

(c) The estimate for the 74,000 units of production is likely to be more accurate than the estimate for 90,000 units. Estimating the costs at 74,000 units is an example of interpolation, in that the estimate is being made for a production level that is within the range of production levels used to estimate the variable and fixed costs. 90,000 units of production is significantly higher than the levels of production used in estimating fixed and variable costs and therefore it is possible that the costs would behave differently at this level of production. This is an example of extrapolation.

Task 1.9

(a) The variable element of the production cost per unit is £ 3 .

(b)

Level of production Units	Fixed cost £
40,000	85,000
48,000	135,000

Working:

	Activity level	Cost £
High	48,000	279,000 – 50,000 = 229,000
Low	40,000	205,000
Increase	8,000	24,000
Variable element = £24,000/8,000		
= £3 per unit		
Fixed element		
At 40,000 units		
Variable element £3 × 40,000 units		120,000
Fixed element (bal fig)		85,000
Total cost		205,000
Fixed element		
At 48,000 units		
Variable element £3 × 48,000 units		144,000
Fixed element (bal fig)		135,000
Total cost		279,000

Task 1.10

(a) Cost of 9,000 units = £ | 64,000 |.

(b) Cost of 11,000 units = £ | 81,000 |.

Working:

Variable cost per unit = $\dfrac{£93,000 - £15,000}{13,000}$ = £6 per unit

Fixed element for activity level up to 9,999 units = £58,000 – (8,000 × £6) = £10,000

Cost at 9,000 units = £10,000 + (9,000 × £6) = £64,000

Cost at 11,000 units = £15,000 + (11,000 × £6) = £81,000

Task 1.11

(a) Cost of 19,000 units = £ | 493,000 |.

(b) Cost of 21,000 units = £ | 545,000 |.

Working:

We have been told that the variable element is £25 per unit so we can find the fixed element from this at each activity level:

Fixed element at 18,000 units = £468,000 – (18,000 × £25) = £18,000

Fixed element at 22,000 units = £570,000 – (22,000 × £25) = £20,000

Therefore:

Cost at 19,000 units = £18,000 + (19,000 × £25) = £493,000

Cost at 21,000 units = £20,000 + (21,000 × £25) = £545,000

Task 1.12

The fixed production overheads were | over-absorbed | by £ | 1,250 |.

Working:

Budgeted overhead absorption rate per unit: $\dfrac{£233,750}{55,000}$ = £4.25

Overhead absorbed = actual production at the standard rate: 57,000 units × £4.25 = £242,250.

Actual fixed costs incurred: £241,000.

£242,250 – £241,000 = £1,250.

Task 1.13

Absorption rate method	Cutting rate £	Finishing rate £	Most appropriate 1, 2 or 3
Rate per unit	5.86	4.24	2 – Most appropriate where all products are of similar size and require a similar input in terms of time and resources of the departments
Rate per direct labour hour	14.65	1.77	3 – Most appropriate in labour intensive departments where most of the overhead relates to labour
Rate per machine hour	4.88	21.20	1 – Most appropriate in a largely mechanised department where most of the overhead relates to machinery costs

Workings

	Cutting	Finishing
Rate per unit	$\dfrac{58,600}{10,000}$	$\dfrac{42,400}{10,000}$
	= £5.86 per unit	= £4.24 per unit
Rate per direct labour hour	$\dfrac{58,600}{4,000}$	$\dfrac{42,400}{24,000}$
	= £14.65 per labour hour	= £1.77 per labour hour
Rate per machine hour	$\dfrac{58,600}{12,000}$	$\dfrac{42,400}{2,000}$
	= £4.88 per machine hour	£21.20 per machine hour

BPP LEARNING MEDIA

Task 1.14

(a)

Department	Overhead absorption rate
C	£1.25 per machine hour
D	£2.25 per direct labour hour

Working:

$$C = \frac{£125,000}{100,000}$$

= £1.25 per machine hour

As C is a highly mechanised department most of the overhead will relate to the machinery therefore machine hours have been used to absorb the overhead.

$$D = \frac{£180,000}{80,000}$$

= £2.25 per direct labour hour

As D is a highly labour intensive department then most of the overhead will relate to the hours that are worked by the labour force therefore labour hours are used to absorb the overhead.

(b) The overhead to be included in the cost of product P is £ | 22,000 |.

Working:

Product P – Department C overhead	£1.25 × 5	= £ 6.25
– Department D overhead	£2.25 × 7	= £15.75
		£22.00

Task 1.15

	£
Overhead apportioned to packaging department	11,429
Overhead apportioned to assembly department	8,571

Working:

Number of employees who use canteen = 20 + 50% × 30 = 35 employees
Cost per employee = £20,000/35 = £571.43 per employee
Therefore, cost apportioned to packaging department = 20 × £571.43 = £11,429
Cost apportioned to assembly department = 15 × £571.43 = £8,571

Task 1.16

	Under-absorption £	Over-absorption £	Debit/Credit
(W1) Budgeted production was 1,200 units and budgeted overheads were £5,400. Overheads are to be absorbed on a unit basis. The actual production was 1,000 units and the overheads incurred were £5,000.	500		Debit
(W2) Budgeted production was 600 units to be produced in 1,800 labour hours. Budgeted overheads of £5,040 are to be absorbed on a direct labour hour basis. The actual production for the period was 700 units in 2,200 labour hours and the actual overheads were £5,100.		1,060	Credit
(W3) Budgeted production was 40,000 units and the budgeted machine hours were 2 hours per unit. Budgeted overheads were £320,000 and were to be absorbed on a machine hour basis. The actual overheads incurred were £320,000 and the production was 42,000 units. The total machine hours were 82,000.		8,000	Credit

Workings

Row 1   Overhead absorption rate $= \dfrac{\pounds5,400}{1,200}$

                                          = £4.50 per unit

        Overhead incurred   = £5,000

        Overhead absorbed

        1,000 units × £4.50   = £4,500

        Under-absorbed overhead = £500 – a further expense in the statement of profit or loss (income statement)

Row 2   Overhead absorption rate $= \dfrac{\pounds5,040}{1,800}$

                                          = £2.80 per direct labour hour

        Overhead incurred   = £5,100

        Overhead absorbed

        2,200 hours × £2.80   = £6,160

        Over-absorbed overhead   = £1,060 – a credit to the statement of profit or loss (income statement)

Row 3   Overhead absorption rate $= \dfrac{\pounds320,000}{80,000}$

                                          = £4.00 per machine hour

        Overhead incurred   = £320,000

        Overhead absorbed

        82,000 × £4.00   = £328,000

        Over-absorbed overhead   = £8,000 – a credit to the statement of profit or loss (income statement)

Task 1.17

The unit cost under absorption costing will be | £ | 39.50 |.

The unit cost under marginal costing will be | £ | 37.50 |.

Workings

1 **Absorption costing**

	£
Direct materials	12.00
Direct labour – Cutting (2 × £7.40)	14.80
Finishing	6.80
Variable overheads:	
Cutting (2 × £1.40)	2.80
Finishing (1 × £1.10)	1.10
Fixed overheads:	
Cutting (2 × £0.60)	1.20
Finishing (1 × £0.80)	0.80
	39.50

2 **Marginal costing**

	£
Direct materials	12.00
Direct labour – Cutting (2 × £7.40)	14.80
Finishing	6.80
Variable overheads:	
Cutting (2 × £1.40)	2.80
Finishing (1 × £1.10)	1.10
	37.50

3   **Hourly absorption rates**

	Rate per hour £
Variable overheads:	
Cutting (£336,000/240,000)	1.40
Finishing (£132,000/120,000)	1.10
Fixed overheads:	
Cutting (£144,000/240,000)	0.60
Finishing (£96,000/120,000)	0.80

Task 1.18

(a) The absorption costing profit for July was   £ | 52,800 .

The absorption costing profit for August was   £ | 60,000 .

The marginal costing profit for July was   £ | 49,100 .

The marginal costing profit for August was   £ | 61,850 .

Workings

1   **Cost per unit – absorption costing**

	£
Direct materials	6.80
Direct labour	3.60
Variable costs (£32,400/24,000)	1.35
Fixed costs (£44,400/24,000)	1.85
	13.60

2 Cost per unit – marginal costing

	£
Direct materials	6.80
Direct labour	3.60
Variable costs (£32,400/24,000)	1.35
	11.75

3 Absorption costing – statement of profit or loss (income statement)

		July £	July £	August £	August £
Sales	(22,000 × £16)		352,000		
	(25,000 × £16)				400,000
Less cost of sales					
Opening inventory	(1,500 × £13.60)	20,400			
	(3,500 × £13.60)			47,600	
Production	(24,000 × £13.60)	326,400		326,400	
		346,800		374,000	
Less closing inventory (3,500 × £13.60)		(47,600)			
	(2,500 × £13.60)			(34,000)	
			299,200		340,000
Profit			52,800		60,000

4 Marginal costing – statement of profit or loss (income statement)

			July £		August £
		£	£	£	£
Sales	(22,000 × £16)		352,000		
	(25,000 × £16)				400,000
Less: cost of sales					
Opening inventory (1,500 × £11.75)		17,625			
	(3,500 × £11.75)			41,125	
Production	(24,000 × £11.75)	282,000		282,000	
		299,625		323,125	
Less: closing inventory	(3,500 × £11.75)	(41,125)			
	(2,500 × £11.75)			(29,375)	
			258,500		293,750
Contribution			93,500		106,250
Fixed costs			(44,400)		(44,400)
			49,100		61,850

(b) Reconciliation of profit figures

		July £	August £
Absorption cost profit		52,800	60,000
Increase in inventory	(3,500 – 1,500)		
× Fixed c.p.u.	2,000 × £1.85	(3,700)	
Decrease in inventory	(3,500 – 2,500)		
× Fixed c.p.u.	1,000 × £1.85		1,850
Marginal cost profit		49,100	61,850

Task 1.19

(a) The profit for the quarter under absorption costing is $£$ | 47,560 | .

The profit for the quarter under marginal costing is $£$ | 48,840 | .

Workings

1 **Unit cost – absorption costing**

	£
Direct materials	23.60
Direct labour (4 × £5.80)	23.20
Variable overheads (£88,000/8,000)	11.00
Fixed overheads (£51,200/8,000)	6.40
	64.20

2 **Unit cost – marginal costing**

	£
Direct materials	23.60
Direct labour (4 × £5.80)	23.20
Variable overheads (£88,000/8,000)	11.00
	57.80

3 **Absorption costing – statement of profit or loss (income statement)**

	£	£
Sales (8,200 × £70)		574,000
Less cost of sales		
Opening inventory (840 × £64.20)	53,928	
Production cost (8,000 × £64.20)	513,600	
	567,528	
Less closing inventory (640 × £64.20)	(41,088)	
		526,440
Profit		47,560

4 Marginal costing – Statement of profit or loss (income statement)

	£	£
Sales (8,200 × £70)		574,000
Less cost of sales		
Opening inventory (840 × £57.80)	48,552	
Production cost (8,000 × £57.80)	462,400	
	510,952	
Less closing inventory (640 × £57.80)	(36,992)	
		473,960
Contribution		100,040
Less fixed costs		(51,200)
Profit		48,840

(b)

	£
Absorption costing profit	47,560
Decrease in inventory × fixed cost per unit (200 × £6.40)	1,280
Marginal costing profit	48,840

Chapter 2

Task 2.1

	Production costs £	Three-month moving total £	Three-month moving average £
March	104,500		
April	110,300	327,600	109,200
May	112,800	332,500	110,833
June	109,400	339,800	113,267
July	117,600	343,000	114,333
August	116,000	352,800	117,600
September	119,200	357,500	119,167
October	122,300	362,000	120,667
November	120,500	362,100	120,700
December	119,300		

Task 2.2

(a)

		Actual £	Five-day moving average trend £	Seasonal variation (actual – trend) £
Week 1	Day 1	600		
	Day 2	700		
	Day 3	1,000	1,000	–
	Day 4	1,200	1,016	+184
	Day 5	1,500	1,026	+474
Week 2	Day 1	680	1,076	–396
	Day 2	750	1,116	–366
	Day 3	1,250	1,188	+ 62
	Day 4	1,400	1,216	+184
	Day 5	1,860	1,272	+588
Week 3	Day 1	820	1,410	–590
	Day 2	1,030	1,550	–520
	Day 3	1,940	1,678	+262
	Day 4	2,100	1,714	+386
	Day 5	2,500	1,772	+728
Week 4	Day 1	1,000	1,696	–696
	Day 2	1,320	1,734	–414
	Day 3	1,560	1,768	–208
	Day 4	2,290		
	Day 5	2,670		

(b)

MEMO

To: Colleague
From: Accounting technician
Date: 7 August 20X5

Subject: Usefulness of trend and seasonal variation figures

Trend

The trend shows how the daily takings have increased each day over the four-week period and the seasonal variations show how the takings on some days of the week are generally lower or higher than on other days of the week. As the restaurant has only just opened and the time series figures are for the first four weeks of operation, the trend figure may not be a good indication of the future trend of the business. The takings appear to be increasing rapidly but this may be due to the fact that the restaurant is new and that customers are trying it out. Only if this trend continues in the longer term will it be a reliable basis for future predictions.

Seasonal variation

The same criticism of the daily seasonal variation can also be made. However, this does at least appear on the whole to be showing the same positive/negative pattern each week, other than on Day 3 when out of the four figures the variation is zero in the first week, negative for two weeks and then positive in week four.

In general in order to be able to use the trend of figures and seasonal variations, a more stable and longer term set of results is necessary.

Task 2.3

		Actual £	Four-quarter moving average £	Centred moving average – trend £	Seasonal variations (actual – trend) £
20X5	Quarter 3	50,600			
	Quarter 4	52,800			
			51,900		

		Actual £	Four-quarter moving average £	Centred moving average – trend £	Seasonal variations (actual – trend) £
20X6	Quarter 1	55,600		51,975	+3,625
			52,050		
	Quarter 2	48,600		52,188	–3,588
			52,325		
	Quarter 3	51,200		52,625	–1,425
			52,925		
	Quarter 4	53,900		53,075	+825
			53,225		
20X7	Quarter 1	58,000		53,450	+4,550
			53,675		
	Quarter 2	49,800		53,763	–3,963
			53,850		
	Quarter 3	53,000		54,113	–1,113
			54,375		
	Quarter 4	54,600		54,488	+112
			54,600		
20X8	Quarter 1	60,100		54,750	+5,350
			54,900		
	Quarter 2	50,700		54,975	–4,275
			55,050		
	Quarter 3	54,200			
	Quarter 4	55,200			

Task 2.4

	Workings	Predicted sales £
Quarter 1	£418,500 + £21,500	440,000
Quarter 2	£420,400 + £30,400	450,800
Quarter 3	£422,500 – £16,700	405,800
Quarter 4	£423,800 – £35,200	388,600

Task 2.5

(a)

	Actual costs £	RPI	Workings	Costs at January prices £
January	129,600	171.1	129,600	129,600
February	129,700	172.0	129,700 × 171.1/172.0	129,021
March	130,400	172.2	130,400 × 171.1/172.2	129,567
April	131,600	173.0	131,600 × 171.1/173.0	130,155
May	130,500	174.1	130,500 × 171.1/174.1	128,251
June	131,600	174.3	131,600 × 171.1/174.3	129,184

(b)

	Actual costs £	RPI	Workings	Costs at June prices £
January	129,600	171.1	129,600 × 174.3/171.1	132,024
February	129,700	172.0	129,700 × 174.3/172.0	131,434
March	130,400	172.2	130,400 × 174.3/172.2	131,990
April	131,600	173.0	131,600 × 174.3/173.0	132,589
May	130,500	174.1	130,500 × 174.3/174.1	130,650
June	131,600	174.3	131,600 × 174.3/174.3	131,600

(c)

> **MEMO**
>
> **To:** Colleague
> **From:** Accounting technician
> **Date:** 7 August 20X5
>
> **Subject:** What the adjusted figures mean
>
> **Cost figures in terms of January prices**
>
> The unadjusted figures show that costs are generally increasing each month. However, when adjusted to January prices using the RPI it can be seen that, other than April, costs are in fact below the January level.
>
> **Cost figures in terms of June prices**
>
> The price adjusted figures show that costs have fallen in real terms over the six-month period.

Task 2.6

		Actual sales £	Workings	Index
20X7	Quarter 1	126,500		100.0
	Quarter 2	130,500	130,500/126,500 × 100	103.2
	Quarter 3	131,400	131,400/126,500 × 100	103.9
	Quarter 4	132,500	132,500/126,500 × 100	104.7
20X8	Quarter 1	133,100	133,100/126,500 × 100	105.2
	Quarter 2	135,600	135,600/126,500 × 100	107.2
	Quarter 3	136,500	136,500/126,500 × 100	107.9
	Quarter 4	137,100	137,100/126,500 × 100	108.4

Task 2.7

The updated standard cost for material C is **£** | 4.41 |.

Working: £3.50 × 145/115 = £4.41

Task 2.8

Quarter 1	£	667,396

Quarter 2	£	722,633

Working:

Quarter 1   £657,000 × 128.4/126.4 = £667,396
Quarter 2   £692,500 × 131.9/126.4 = £722,633

Task 2.9

	£
January 20X9	12.10
February 20X9	12.20

Workings

1   **Expected price in January**

a = 9
b = 0.1
X = 31

Therefore Y = 9 + (0.1 × 31) = £12.10 per kilogram

2   **Expected price in February**

a = 9
b = 0.1
X = 32

Therefore Y = 9 + (0.1 × 32) = £12.20 per kilogram

Task 2.10

a is	£	£2,000

b is	£	£5

If production is 750 units, the cost of production is | £ | 5,750 |.

Working:

100 units   £2,500
1,000 units   £7,000

Subtract the highest less the lowest activities to find the variable cost which is b in the equation:

1,000 – 100 = 900 units with additional cost of £(7,000 – 2,500) = £4,500, ie £4,500/900 per unit = £5 per unit

b = £5

Therefore, to find the fixed cost element, consider 100 units:

Fixed costs = Total costs – Variable costs

= £2,500 – 5 × 100

= £2,000

So a = £2,000

Task 2.11

If production is expected to be 105,000 units in the next quarter the anticipated production costs are £ | 810,000 .

Working:

Production costs = 138,000 + (6.4 × 105,000)

= £810,000

Task 2.12

The anticipated power costs for April are £ | 270,000 .

Working: Power costs 80,000 + (380,000 × 0.5) = £270,000

Task 2.13

Month 1 = 25,600 units

Month 2 = 26,500 units

Month 3 = 27,400 units

Working:

Month 1: sales trend = 3.1 + (0.9 × 25) (month 25)
= 25,600 units

Month 2: sales trend = 3.1 + (0.9 × 26)
= 26,500 units

Month 3: sales trend = 3.1 + (0.9 × 27)
= 27,400 units

Task 2.14

Quarter 1 = | 1,590 | units

Quarter 2 = | 2,095 | units

Quarter 3 = | 2,125 | units

Quarter 4 = | 1,880 | units

Workings

	Trend			Seasonal variation			Estimate of actual
Quarter 1	400 + (105 × 13)*	=		1,765 – 175	=		1,590
Quarter 2	400 + (105 × 14)	=		1,870 + 225	=		2,095
Quarter 3	400 + (105 × 15)	=		1,975 + 150	=		2,125
Quarter 4	400 + (105 × 16)	=		2,080 – 200	=		1,880

*x = 13.

Q1 20X6 – Q4 20X8 = 12 quarters

Therefore, Q1 20X6 – Q1 20X9 = 13
Q1 20X6 – Q2 20X9 = 14
Q1 20X6 – Q3 20X9 = 15
Q1 20X6 – Q4 20X9 = 16

Task 2.15

(a)

	£
June cost per tonne	177
July cost per tonne	179

Working:

$y = a + bx$

For June, x = 26, therefore y = 125 + (2 × 26) = £177 per tonne

For July = x = 27, therefore y = 125 + (2 × 27) = £179 per tonne

(b)

June index	101.14
July index	102.29

Working:

As May is the base, May = 100 when price was £175 per tonne

Therefore,   June = 177/175 × 100 = 101.14

                    July = 179/175 × 100 = 102.29

··

Task 2.16

(a)

	£
a	10,000
b	3

Working:

Substituting the outputs and corresponding distribution costs into the equation gives:

£14,500 = a + 1,500 b
£19,000 = a + 3,000 b

Subtracting the two equations gives:

£4,500 = 1,500 b
b = £3 per unit

Substituting this into the first equation gives:

£14,500 = a + 1,500 × £3
a = £10,000

(b)

Output	£
2,000 units (£10,000 + £3 × 2,000)	16,000
4,000 units (£10,000 + £3 × 4,000)	22,000

(c) The value of distribution costs for | 2,000 | units is most accurate.

Note. This is because this is within the range of the activities (1,500 – 3,000) which were used to determine a and b in the equation (interpolation). 4,000 units is an activity outside the range (and so requires extrapolation).

Task 2.17

(a) The trend in prices is | a decrease | of | **£** | 25 | per month.

The seasonal variation for month 1 is | a decrease | of

| **£** | 55 |.

Working:

£1,040 – **£25** = £1,015
£1,015 – **£25** = £990
£1,040 – £985 = £55

(b)

| a = £ | 12,000 |
| b = £ | 5 |

Working:

1: 52,000 = a + (b × 8,000)
2: 72,000 = a + (b × 12,000)
3: 79,500 = a + (b × 13,500)

Equation 2 less equation 1 gives:

20,000 = (b × 4,000)
b = £5

Substitute b in equation 3

79,500 = a + (5 × 13,500)
79,500 = a + 67,500
a = £12,000

Alternatively you could have used the high-low method to calculate a and b.

(c)

Month	Index number	Forecast hourly rate £
March	103.9	12.47
April	105.2	12.62
May	105.7	12.68

Working:

Index base 100 = £12

$$\left(\frac{103.9}{100}\right) \times £12 = £12.47$$

$$\left(\frac{105.2}{100}\right) \times £12 = £12.62$$

$$\left(\frac{105.7}{100}\right) \times £12 = £12.68$$

(d) The forecast total hour cost for April is   **£**   24,230.40   .

Working: 1,920 × £12.62 = £24,230.40

Chapter 3

Task 3.1

	✓
£41.40	
£53.40	
£83.40	
£98.40	✓

Workings

	£	£
Materials		
A 1.2 kg × £11 =	13.20	
B 4.7 kg × £6 =	28.20	
		41.40
Labour		
1.5 hours × £8		12.00
Prime cost		53.40
Overheads		
1.5 hours × £30		45.00
Standard cost per unit		98.40

Task 3.2

One unit of XX6	Quantity	Cost per unit £	Total £
Materials	1.25	1.65	2.06
Labour	0.25	17.00	4.25
Fixed overheads	1.00	5.50	5.50
Total			11.81

Workings

Standard materials quantity per unit of XX6: $\dfrac{17,500}{14,000}$ = 1.25 litres

Standard labour quantity per unit of XX6: $\dfrac{3,500}{14,000}$ = 0.25 hours

Standard fixed overhead units: Fixed overheads absorbed on a unit basis = 1

Standard materials cost per litre: $\dfrac{£28,875}{17,500}$ = £1.65

Standard labour rate per hour: $\dfrac{£59,500}{3,500}$ = £17.00

Fixed overheads cost per unit: $\dfrac{£77,000}{14,000}$ = £5.50

Materials total cost per unit of XX6: $\dfrac{£28,875}{14,000}$ = £2.06

Labour total cost per unit of XX6: $\dfrac{£59,500}{14,000}$ = £4.25

Fixed overheads total cost per unit of XX6: $\dfrac{£77,000}{14,000}$ = £5.50

Task 3.3

(a) The standard quantity of labour per unit is ⟨ 15 ⟩ minutes.

(b) The budgeted quantity of materials needed to produce 13,500 units of X07 is ⟨ 16,875 ⟩ litres.

(c) The budgeted labour hours to produce 12,000 units of X07 is ⟨ 3,000 ⟩ hours.

(d) The budgeted labour cost to produce 13,500 units of X07 is
⟨ £ 57,375 ⟩.

(e) The budgeted overhead absorption rate per unit is ⟨ £ 5.50 ⟩.

(f) The fixed production overheads were ⟨ under-absorbed ⟩ by
⟨ £ 4,080 ⟩.

Workings

1   3,500 direct labour hours/14,000 units = 0.25 hours (15 minutes).

2   Budgeted quantity per unit = 17,500 litres/14,000 units = 1.25 litres

       13,500 units × 1.25 litres = 16,875 litres

3   Budgeted labour hours per unit = 0.25 hours (see part (a))

       12,000 units × 0.25 hours = 3,000 hours

4   Budgeted labour cost per unit = £59,500/14,000 units = £4.25

       13,500 units × £4.25 hours = £57,375

5   Budgeted OAR = £77,000/14,000 units = £5.50 per unit

6   Budgeted OAR = £436,250/25,000 units = £17.45 per unit

       Overheads absorbed = 27,000 units × £17.45 = £471,150

Actual fixed costs	£475,230
Under absorbed	£4,080

Task 3.4

Standard cost card for per unit of Plate	£
Direct materials (2 × £3.50)	7.00
Direct labour – grade A (0.5 × £15)	7.50
Direct labour – grade B (0.25 × £10)	2.50
Fixed overhead (£100,000/20,000)	5.00
Total standard cost per unit	22.00

Chapter 4

Task 4.1

	Variance £	Adverse/Favourable
Total materials cost variance	4,480	Adverse
Materials price variance	2,880	Adverse
Materials usage variance	1,600	Adverse

Workings

1 **Total materials cost variance**

	£
Standard cost of actual production 2,800 units × 5 kg × £4.00	56,000
Actual cost	60,480
Total cost variance	4,480 (A)

2 **Materials price variance**

	£
14,400 kg should have cost (× £4.00)	57,600
But did cost	60,480
Price variance	2,880 (A)

3 **Materials usage variance**

2,800 units should have used × 5 kg	14,000 kg
But did use	14,400 kg
	400 kg
At standard cost	× £4.00
Usage variance	£1,600 (A)

Task 4.2

	Variance £	Adverse/Favourable
Total materials cost variance	13,680	Adverse
Materials price variance	16,080	Adverse
Materials usage variance	2,400	Favourable

Workings

1 **Total materials cost variance**

	£
Standard cost for actual production 11,400 units × 4 kg × £3	136,800
Actual cost	150,480
Total cost variance	13,680 (A)

2 **Materials price variance**

	£
44,800 kg should have cost (× £3)	134,400
But did cost	150,480
Price variance	16,080 (A)

3 **Materials usage variance**

	£
11,400 units should have used (× 4 kg)	45,600
But did use	44,800
	800 (F)
At standard cost	× £3
Usage variance	2,400 (F)

Task 4.3

	Variance £	Adverse/Favourable
Total labour cost variance	12,715	Adverse
Labour rate variance	9,430	Adverse
Labour efficiency variance	3,285	Adverse

Workings

1   **Total labour cost variance**

	£
Standard cost for actual production 12,100 units × 4.5 hours × £7.30	397,485
Actual cost	410,200
Total cost variance	12,715 (A)

2   **Labour rate variance**

	£
54,900 hours should have cost (× £7.30)	400,770
But did cost	410,200
Rate variance	9,430 (A)

3   **Labour efficiency variance**

12,100 units should have taken (× 4.5 hours)	54,450 hrs
But did take	54,900 hrs
	450 hrs (A)
At standard rate	× £7.30
Efficiency variance	£3,285 (A)

Task 4.4

	Variance £	Adverse/Favourable
Total labour cost variance	2,200	Favourable
Labour rate variance	4,200	Favourable
Labour efficiency variance	2,000	Adverse

Workings

1   **Total labour cost variance**

	£
Standard cost for actual production 10,680 units × 5 hours × £10	534,000
Actual cost	531,800
Total cost variance	2,200 (F)

2   **Labour rate variance**

	£
53,600 hours should have cost (× £10)	536,000
But did cost	531,800
Rate variance	4,200 (F)

3   **Labour efficiency variance**

10,680 units should have taken (× 5 hours)	53,400 hrs
But did take	53,600 hrs
	200 hrs (A)
At standard rate	× £10
Efficiency variance	£2,000 (A)

Task 4.5

	Variance £	Adverse/Favourable
Direct labour rate	2,500	Adverse
Direct labour efficiency	2,800	Favourable
Idle time	700	Adverse

Workings

1   **Labour rate variance**

	£
2,300 hours should have cost (× £7)	16,100
But did cost	18,600
Rate variance	2,500 (A)

2   **Labour efficiency variance**

260 units should have taken (× 10 hours)	2,600 hrs
But did take	2,200 hrs
	400 hrs (F)
At standard rate × £7	× £7
Efficiency variance	£2,800 (F)

3   **Idle time variance**

	£
Idle time hours at standard rate (100 hours × £7)	700 (A)

Task 4.6

	Variance £	Adverse/Favourable
Idle time variance	2,700	Adverse

Working:

	£
Idle time hours at standard rate (300 hours × £9)	2,700 (A)

Task 4.7

	Variance £	Adverse/Favourable
Total labour cost variance	8,600	Adverse
Labour rate variance	4,100	Adverse
Labour efficiency variance	4,500	Adverse

Workings

1 **Total labour cost variance**

	£
Standard cost for actual production 11,400 × 3 hours × £9	307,800
Actual cost	316,400
Total variance	8,600 (A)

2 **Labour rate variance**

	£
34,700 hours should have cost (× £9)	312,300
But did cost	316,400
Rate variance	4,100 (A)

3   Labour efficiency variance

11,400 units should have taken (× 3 hours)	34,200 hrs
But did take	34,700 hrs
	500 hrs (A)
At standard rate × £9	× £9
Efficiency variance	£4,500 (A)

Task 4.8

The fixed overhead expenditure variance is $\boxed{£ \quad £5,000}$ Adverse.

The fixed overhead volume variance is $\boxed{£ \quad 10,500}$ Favourable.

Workings

1   **Fixed overhead expenditure variance**

	£
Budgeted overhead £7 × 10,000 units	70,000
Actual overhead	75,000
Expenditure variance	5,000 (A)

2   **Fixed overhead volume variance**

	£
Actual production @ standard OAR 11,500 × £7	80,500
Budgeted production @ standard OAR 10,000 × £7	70,000
Volume variance	10,500 (F)

Task 4.9

		Adverse/Favourable
Division A Fixed overhead expenditure variance (£)	80,000	Favourable
Division A Fixed overhead volume variance (£)	91,200	Favourable
Division B Total materials used (kg)	98,000	
Division B Material usage variance (kg)	1,750	

Workings

1 **Division A Fixed overhead expenditure variance**

	£
Budgeted fixed overhead 50,000 units × 6 hours × £7.60	2,280,000
Actual fixed overhead	2,200,000
Expenditure variance	80,000 (F)

2 **Division A Fixed overhead volume variance**

	£
Standard hours for actual production @ standard OAR 52,000 units × 6 hours × £7.60	2,371,200
Standard hours for budgeted production @ standard OAR 50,000 units × 6 hours × £7.60	2,280,000
Volume variance	91,200 (F)

3 **Division B Total materials purchased in kg**

	£
Actual materials purchased should cost (balancing figure)	529,200
Actual materials used did cost (per question)	515,680
Materials price variance (per question)	13,520 (F)

Total materials used in kg = £529,200/£5.40 = 98,000 kg

4   **Division B Material usage variance in kg**

Material usage variance in kg: £9,450/£5.40 = 1,750 kg (A)

Task 4.10

(a) The budgeted fixed overhead for the month was

£ | 201,600 .

(b) The fixed overhead expenditure variance was

£ | 1,400 | Adverse.

(c) The fixed overhead volume variance was £ | 11,520 | Adverse.

(d) The number of labour hours worked in June was 53,000 hours.

(e) The labour efficiency variance in hours for June was 1,700 Adverse.

Workings

1   **Budgeted fixed overhead**

	£
Budgeted fixed overhead 14,000 units × 4 hours × £3.60	201,600

2   **Fixed overhead expenditure variance**

	£
Budgeted fixed overhead	201,600
Actual fixed overhead	203,000
Expenditure variance	1,400 (A)

3   **Fixed overhead volume variance**

	£
Standard hours for actual production @ standard OAR 13,200 units × 4 hours × £3.60	190,080
Standard hours for budgeted production @ standard OAR 14,000 units × 4 hours × £3.60	201,600
Volume variance	11,520 (A)

4   **The labour efficiency variance in hours for June was**

Labour efficiency variance in hours: £13,600/£8 = 1,700 hours adverse (adverse given in question)

5   **Number of labour hours worked in June**

Labour efficiency variance (above) = 1,700 hours	
25,650 units should take (25,650 units × 2 hrs)	51,300 hrs
25,650 units did take (balancing figure)	53,000 hrs
Variance in hours	1,700 (A)

Task 4.11

(a)

	£
Budgeted fixed overhead expenditure (4,100 × 40 × £12.50)	2,050,000
Actual fixed overhead expenditure	2,195,000
Fixed overhead **expenditure variance**	145,000 (A)

(b)

	£
Actual production at standard rate (3,850 × 40 × £12.50)	1,925,000
Budgeted production at standard rate (4,100 × 40 × £12.50)	2,050,000
Fixed overhead **volume variance**	125,000 (A)

Task 4.12

	Variance £	Adverse/Favourable
Total variable production overhead variance	30	Adverse
Variable production overhead efficiency variance	60	Favourable
Variable production overhead expenditure variance	90	Adverse

Workings

1 **Total variable production overhead variance**

	£
400 units of product X should cost (× £3)	1,200
But did cost	1,230
Variable production overhead total variance	30 (A)

2 **Variable overhead expenditure variance**

	£
760 hours of variable production overhead should cost (× £1.50)	1,140
But did cost	1,230
Variable production overhead expenditure variance	90 (A)

3   **Variable overhead efficiency variance**

400 units of product X should take (× 2hrs)	800 hrs
But did take	760 hrs
Variable production overhead efficiency variance in hours	40 hrs (F)
× standard rate per hour	× £1.50
Variable production overhead efficiency variance in £	£60 (F)

Task 4.13

(a)   The variable production cost variance is

£	£208,000	Adverse.

Working:

This is simply a 'total' variance.

	£
1,000 units should have cost (× £600)	600,000
But did cost (£720,000 + £63,000 + £25,000)	808,000
Variable production cost variance	208,000 (A)

(b)   (i)   The direct labour rate variance is | £ | 2,600 | Favourable.

Working:

	£
8,200 hours should cost (× £8)	65,600
But did cost	63,000
Direct labour rate variance	2,600 (F)

BPP
LEARNING MEDIA

(ii) The direct labour efficiency variance is £ | 14,400 | Favourable.

Working:

1,000 units should take (× 10 hours)	10,000 hrs
But did take	8,200 hrs
Direct labour efficiency variance in hrs	1,800 hrs (F)
× standard rate per hour	× £8
Direct labour efficiency variance in £	14,400 (F)

(c) **(i)** The direct material price variance is £ | 270,000 | Adverse.

Working:

	£
90,000 kg should cost (× £5)	450,000
But did cost	720,000
Direct material price variance	270,000 (A)

(ii) The direct material usage variance is £ | 50,000 | Favourable.

Working:

1,000 units should use (× 100 kg)	100,000 kg
But did use	90,000 kg
Direct material usage variance in kg	10,000 kg (F)
× standard cost per kg	× £5
Direct material usage variance in £	£50,000 (F)

(d) **(i)** The variable production overhead expenditure variance

is £ | £8,600 | Adverse.

Working:

	£
8,200 hours incurring o/hd should cost (× £2)	16,400
But did cost	25,000
Variable production overhead expenditure variance	8,600 (A)

(ii) The variable production overhead efficiency variance is

£ | 3,600 | Favourable.

Working:

Efficiency variance in hrs (from (b)(ii))	1,800 hrs (F)
× standard rate per hour	× £2
Variable production overhead efficiency variance	£3,600 (F)

Task 4.14

Standard cost per kg = £ | £2.85

Actual material purchased should cost (balancing figure)	193,800
Actual material purchased did cost	197,600
	3,800 A

£193,800/68,000 kg = £ | £2.85 | per kg

Standard kg of material per units = 3 kg

Material usage variance in kg: £2,850/£2.85 = 1,000 kg F

Actual production should use (balancing figure)	69,000 kg
Actual production did use	68,000 kg
Variance in kg	1,000 F

Standard usage per unit = 69,000 kg/23,000 units = 3 kg

Task 4.15

(a) The material usage variance is £ | 6,000 | adverse .

19,000 units should use (× 10 litres per unit)	190,000 litres
But did use	200,000 litres
Material usage variance in litres	10,000 litres (A)
× standard cost per litre (£132,000/220,000 litres)	× £0.60
Material usage variance in £	6,000 (A)

(b) The total labour efficiency variance is £ | 4,500

favourable .

Working:

Labour efficiency variance

12,000 units should have taken (× 0.6 hours)	7,200 hrs
But did take	6,900 hrs
	300 hrs (F)
At standard rate	× £15.00
Efficiency variance	4,500 (F)

Task 4.16

(a) The fixed overhead volume variance is £ | 25,000

favourable .

	£
Actual production @ standard OAR 30,000 × £12.50	375,000
Budgeted production @ standard OAR 28,000 × £12.50	350,000
Volume variance	25,000 (F)

(b) The actual fixed production overheads incurred were £ | 315,000 .

	£
Budgeted overhead	350,000
Actual overhead (Balancing figure)	315,000
Expenditure variance	35,000 (F)

(c)

Variance	Amount £	Sign
Total variable production overhead variance	50	Favourable
Variable overhead expenditure variance	75	Adverse

Workings

1 **Total variable production overhead variance**

	£
750 units of product RPB should cost (× £5)	3,750
But did cost	3,700
Variable production overhead total variance	50 (F)

2 **Variable overhead expenditure variance**

	£
1,450 hours of variable production overhead should cost (× £2.50)	3,625
But did cost	3,700
Variable production overhead expenditure variance	75 (A)

Task 4.17

Variance	Amount £	Adverse/ Favourable
Direct material usage variance	2,025	Adverse
Direct material price variance	3,120	Adverse
Total direct labour variance	1,305	Favourable

Workings

1   **Direct material usage variance**

Budgeted direct material per unit of KK1: $\dfrac{9,000\,\text{kg}}{18,000\,\text{units}} = 0.5\,\text{kg}$

Budgeted direct material price per kg: $\dfrac{£60,750}{9,000} = £6.75$

15,000 units should have used (× 0.5kg)	7,500 kg
But did use	7,800 kg
Variance in kg	300 kg (A)
× standard cost per kg	× £6.75
Variance in £	2,025 (A)

2   **Direct material price variance**

	£
7,800 kg should have cost (× £6.75)	52,650
But did cost	55,770
Direct material price variance	3,120 (A)

3   **Total direct labour variance**

Standard hours per unit $\dfrac{5,400\,\text{hrs}}{18,000\,\text{units}} = 0.3$ hours per unit

Standard labour cost per hour $\dfrac{47,250}{5,400\,\text{hrs}} = £8.75$ per hr

Therefore one unit should cost 0.3 hours × £8.75 = £2.625

	£
Actual production should have cost 15,000 units × £2.625	39,375
But did cost	38,070
Variance	1,305 (F)

Task 4.18

(a)

Variance	Amount £	Sign
Fixed overhead expenditure	96,250	Favourable
Fixed overhead volume	83,500	Favourable

Working:

Fixed overhead expenditure variance: (£1,043,750 – £947,500) = £96,250 Favourable

Fixed overhead expenditure budgeted absorption rate: $\dfrac{£1,043,750}{25,000}$ = £41.75 per unit

Fixed overhead volume variance: (27,000 units – 25,000 units) × £41.75 = £83,500 Favourable

(b)

Variance	Amount £	Sign
Variable overhead expenditure variance	250	Favourable
Variable overhead efficiency variance	875	Favourable

Workings

1 **Variable overhead expenditure variance**

	£
3,050 hours of variable production overhead should cost (× £5)	15,250
But did cost	15,000
Variable production overhead expenditure variance	250 (F)

2   Variable overhead efficiency variance

1,075 units of ZX250 should take (× 3hrs)	3,225 hrs
But did take	3,050 hrs
Variable production overhead efficiency variance in hours	175 hrs (F)
× standard rate per hour	× £5
Variable production overhead efficiency variance in £	£875 (F)

Task 4.19

The actual quantity of material used is [51] kg.

The standard labour rate is £ [13] per hour.

Workings

The first thing to do with questions like these is to lay out variances in the way you would normally calculate them and then fill in the numbers that the question has given you.

We are given the materials price variance and the actual cost of material so we can start as if we were calculating the materials price variance:

1   Direct material price variance

	£
Actual kg used should have cost (× £15)	A
But did cost	615
Direct material price variance	150 (F)

Now we need to think about what number A must be to give a favourable variance of £150. If the variance is favourable then the actual cost ('did cost') was lower than it should be. This means we need to add £150 to £615 to get 'should cost'. So the materials should have cost £150 + £615 = £765.

We also know that:

Actual kg used should have cost (× £15) = £765

Now we can work out how many kg we actually used: £765/£15 = 51 kg

We can do the same for the labour rate variance.

2   **Labour rate variance**

	£
575 hrs should have cost (× standard rate)	B
But did cost	7,835
Rate variance	360 (A)

Now we need to think about what number B must be to give an adverse variance of £360. If the variance is adverse then the actual cost ('did cost') was higher than it should be. This means we need to deduct £360 from £7,835 to get 'should cost'. So the materials should have cost £7,835 – £360 = £7,475.

We also know that:

575 hrs should have cost (× standard rate) = £7,475

Now we can work out what the standard rate was: £7,475/575 = £13 per hour

Task 4.20

The standard material price is | £ | 3.40 | per kg.

Working:

Direct material price variance

	£
6,850 kg used should have cost (× standard cost)	A
But did cost	21,920
Direct material price variance	1,370 (F)

Now we need to think about what number A must be to give a favourable variance of £1,370. If the variance is favourable then the actual cost ('did cost') was lower than it should be. This means we need to add £1,379 to £21,920 to get 'should cost'. So the materials should have cost £1,370 + £21,920 = £23,290.

We also know that:

6,850 kg used should have cost (× standard cost) = £23,290

Now we can work out what the standard rate was: £23,290/6,850 = £3.40 per kg

BPP
LEARNING MEDIA

Task 4.21

The standard cost per kilogram is £ | 2.50 .

Working:

£10,915 – £1,665 = £9,250 standard cost

Standard cost per kilogram = £9,250/3,700 kilograms = £2.50

Task 4.22

The actual labour rate per hour is £ | 13.25 .

Working:

Standard labour rate per hour: $\dfrac{£163,125}{11,250}$ = £14.50 hr

Actual production at standard labour rate: 11,880 × £14.50 = £172,260

Adjust for the variance: £172,260 – £14,850 = £157,410

Calculate actual rate based on actual hours: $\dfrac{£157,410}{11,880}$ = £13.25 hr

Task 4.23

The quantity of material X used in March 20X4 is 157,000 kg.

Working:

Standard material cost of actual production 6,250 × 25 kg × £10	£1,562,500
Usage variance (adverse)	£7,500
So actual material used actually cost (at standard price per kg)	£1,570,000
÷ Standard price per kg	÷ £10
Actual material used	157,000 kg

Chapter 5

Task 5.1

(a) **(i)** Standard price of fuel = £497,664/1,244,160 litres = £0.40 per litre

(ii) Standard litres of fuel per crossing = 1,244,160/6,480 = 192 litres

Standard litres of fuel for 5,760 crossings = 192 × 5,760 = 1,105,920 litres

(iii) Standard labour rate per hr = £699,840/93,312 hrs = £7.50 per hour

(iv) Standard labour hours per crossing = 93,312/6,480 = 14.4 hours

Standard labour hours for 5,760 crossings = 14.4 × 5,760 = 82,944 hours

(v) Standard fixed overhead cost per budgeted operating hour = £466,560/7,776 = £60 per hour

(vi) Standard operating hours per crossing = 7,776/6,480 = 1.2 hours

Standard operating hours for 5,760 crossings = 1.2 × 5,760 = 6,912 hours

(vii) Standard fixed overhead cost absorbed by 5,760 crossings = 6,912 hours (6) × £60 per hour (from (v)) = £414,720

(b) **(i)**

	£
1,232,800 litres should cost (× £0.40 (a)(i))	493,120
But did cost	567,088
Material price variance for fuel	73,968 (A)

(ii)

	£
5,760 crossings should have used ((a)(ii))	1,105,920 litres
But did use	1,232,800 litres
Usage variance in litres	126,880 litres (A)
× standard price per litre ((a)(i))	× £0.40
Material usage variance for fuel	£50,752 (A)

(iii)

	£
89,856 hours should have cost (× £7.50 (a)(iii))	673,920
But did cost	696,384
Labour rate variance	22,464 (A)

(iv)

5,760 crossing should have used ((a)(iv))	82,944 hours
But did take	89,856 hours
Efficiency variance in hours	6,912 hours (A)
× standard rate per hours ((a)(iii))	× £7.50
Labour efficiency variance	£51,840 (A)

(v)

	£
Budgeted fixed overhead expenditure	466,560
Actual fixed overhead expenditure	472,440
Fixed overhead expenditure variance	5,880 (A)

(vi)

	£
Actual number of crossings (5,760) at standard rate ((a)(vii)	414,720
Budgeted number of crossings at standard rate	466,560
Fixed overhead volume variance	51,840 (A)

(c) **Statement reconciling the actual cost of operations to the standard cost of operations for year ended 30 November 20X8**

Number of ferry crossings		5,760
	£	£
Actual cost of operations		1,735,912
Cost variances	**Adverse**	
Material price for fuel	73,968	
Material usage for fuel	50,752	
Labour rate	22,464	
Labour efficiency	51,840	
Fixed overhead expenditure	5,880	
Fixed overhead volume	51,840	
		256,744 (A)
Standard cost of operations		1,479,168*

* Check. 5,760/6,480 × £1,664,064 = £1,479,168

Task 5.2

(a)

	Favourable £	Adverse £	£
Budgeted variable cost for actual production			387,600
Budgeted fixed cost			234,000
Total budgeted cost for actual production			621,600
Variance	**Favourable £**	**Adverse £**	
Direct materials price	18,700		
Direct materials usage	11,900		
Direct labour rate		28,560	
Direct labour efficiency		12,240	
Fixed overhead expenditure	13,000		
Fixed overhead volume	N/A	N/A	
Total variance	43,600	40,800	(2,800)
Actual cost of actual production			618,800

Working:

Budgeted variable cost per unit = (£130,200 + £223,200)/12,400 units = £28.50

Budgeted variable cost for actual production = £13,600 units × £28.50 = £387,600

Total budgeted cost for actual production = £387,600 + £234,000 (fixed costs) = £621,600

Direct labour efficiency variance

13,600 units should have taken (× 2 hours)	27,200 hrs
But did take	28,560 hrs
	1,360 hrs (A)
At standard rate	× £9.00
Efficiency variance	£12,240 (A)

Fixed overhead expenditure variance = Actual £13,000 lower than budgeted, so favourable.

(b) The under-absorption of overheads is **£** 48,600 .

	£
Overheads absorbed 25,000 × £95	2,375,000
Actual overheads	2,423,600
Under absorbed	48,600

Task 5.3

Operating statement – PD98

			£
Budgeted/Standard cost for actual production			70,824
Variances	**Adverse £**	**Favourable £**	
Direct materials price	5,070		
Direct materials usage		3,120	
Direct labour rate	2,964		
Direct labour efficiency		3,120	
Fixed overhead expenditure	3,220		
Fixed overhead volume		4,368	
Total variance	11,254	10,608	646
Actual cost of actual production			71,470

Working:

Budgeted/Standard cost for actual production, $\left(\dfrac{£61,290}{450}\right) \times 520 = £70,824$

Direct materials price variance: given in the question.

Direct materials usage variance:

520 units should use $\left(\dfrac{337.5\,kg}{450} = 0.75\,kg\right) = 390\,kg$

But did use	338 kg
Variance in kg	52 kg (F)

Therefore, the variance in the question is favourable.

Direct labour rate variance:

$$\frac{£12,960}{1,080} = £12 \text{ hr}$$

Actual hours should cost (£12 × 988)	£11,856
But did cost	£14,820
	£2,964 (A)

Therefore, the £2,964 variance, as provided in the question, is Adverse.

Direct labour efficiency variance: given in the question.

Fixed overhead expenditure variance: £3,220 figure given in question. Variance is Adverse as the £31,300 Actual figure is higher than the £28,080 Budget figure.

Fixed overhead volume variance: given in the question.

···

Task 5.4

			£
Budgeted cost of actual production 1,240 × £38.69			47,976
Variances	**Favourable £**	**Adverse £**	
Materials price		860	
Materials usage	426		
Labour rate	820		
Labour efficiency		1,530	
Fixed overhead expenditure		250	
Fixed overhead volume	560		
Total variances	1,806	2,640	834
Actual cost of actual production (17,100 + 27,060 + 4,650)			48,810

···

Task 5.5

(a)

			£
Standard cost of materials for actual production			114,000
Variances	**Favourable £**	**Adverse £**	
Direct material price variance		45,600	
Direct material usage variance	22,800		
Total variance			22,800
Actual cost of materials for actual production			136,800

Working:

Standard cost for actual units produced = 11,400 units × 5 kg × £2 = £114,000

Materials price variance	£
45,600 kg should have cost (× £2)	91,200
But did cost	136,800
Price variance	45,600 (A)

Materials usage variance	
11,400 units should have used (× 5 kg)	57,000 kg
But did use	45,600
	11,400 (F)
At standard price per kg	× £2
Usage variance	22,800 (F)

(b)

	£		£
Standard cost of labour for actual production			182,400

Variances	Favourable £	Adverse £	
Direct labour rate variance	11,400		
Direct labour efficiency variance	91,200		
Total variance			(102,600)
Actual cost of labour for actual production			79,800

Working:

Standard cost for actual units produced = 11,400 units × 2 hrs × £8 = £182,400

Labour rate variance	£
11,400 hrs should have cost (× £8)	91,200
But did cost	79,800
Rate variance	11,400 (F)

Labour efficiency variance	
11,400 units should have taken (× 2 hours)	22,800 hrs
But did take	11,400 hrs
	11,400 (F)
At standard cost	× £8
Usage variance	91,200 (F)

(c)

			£
Standard cost of fixed overhead for actual production			91,200
Variances	**Favourable £**	**Adverse £**	
Fixed overhead expenditure variance	1,000		
Fixed overhead volume variance		4,800	
Total variance			3,800
Actual cost of fixed overhead for actual production			95,000

Working:

Standard cost for actual units produced = 11,400 units × 2hrs × £4 = £91,200

	£
Budgeted fixed overhead expenditure (12,000 × 2 × £4)	96,000
Actual fixed overhead expenditure	95,000
Fixed overhead **expenditure variance**	1,000 (F)

	£
Standard hours for actual production @ standard OAR 11,400 units × 2 hours × £4	91,200
Standard hours for budgeted production @ standard OAR 12,000 units × 2 hours × £4	96,000
Volume variance	4,800 (A)

Task 5.6

MEMO

To: Managing Director
From: Assistant Management Accountant
Date: xx/xx/xx
Subject: The use of standard marginal costing at Finchley Ltd

As discussed at our earlier meetings, because all companies within the Hampstead Group use standard marginal costing, Finchley Ltd will need to adopt the system from 1 August 20X8. This memo is intended to demonstrate and describe the use of standard marginal costing in your company.

(i)   (1)   Standard marginal cost of a unit of Alpha

	£
Material (36,000m/12,000) 3m × (£432,000/36,000) £12 per m	36.00
Labour (72,000 hrs/12,000) 6 hrs × (£450,000/72,000) £6.25 per hr	37.50
	73.50

(2)   Standard marginal cost of producing 10,000 units of Alpha

	£
Material (£36 × 10,000)	360,000
Labour (£37.50 × 10,000)	375,000
Standard marginal cost	735,000
Fixed overheads	396,000
Total cost	1,131,000

(ii)   (1)

	£
32,000 m should have cost (× £12)	384,000
But did cost	377,600
Material price variance	6,400 (F)

(2)

10,000 units should have used (× 3 m)	30,000 m
But did use	32,000 m
Material usage variance in metres	2,000 m (A)
× standard cost per metre	× £12
Material usage variance in £	24,000 (A)

(3)

	£
70,000 hrs should have cost (× £6.25)	437,500
But did cost	422,800
Labour rate variance	14,700 (F)

(4)

10,000 units should have taken (× 6 hrs)	60,000 hrs
But did take	70,000 hrs
Efficiency variance in hours	10,000 hrs (A)
× standard rate per hour	× £6.25
Labour efficiency variance in £	62,500 (A)

(5)

	£
Budgeted fixed overhead expenditure	396,000
Actual fixed overhead expenditure (£330,000 + £75,000)	405,000
Fixed overhead expenditure variance	9,000 (A)

(iii) Set out below is a statement reconciling the standard cost of production for the three months ended 31 May 20X8 with the actual cost of production for that period.

	Fav £	Adv £	£
Standard cost of output ((see (a)(i)(2))			1,131,000
Variances	**Fav £**	**Adv £**	
Material price	6,400		
Material usage		24,000	
Labour rate	14,700		
Labour efficiency		62,500	
Fixed overhead expenditure		9,000	
	21,100	95,500	74,400 (A)
Actual cost of output			1,205,400

(iv) The total labour variance in the statement above (£47,800 (A)) differs from that in your absorption costing management report for the three months ended 31 May 20X8 because the original report compares the actual cost of producing 10,000 units and the budgeted cost of producing 12,000 units. It, therefore, fails to compare like with like. The report above, however, compares actual costs of producing 10,000 units and what costs should have been given the actual output of 10,000 units. The total material variances in the two reports also differ for this reason. There is very little point comparing a budgeted cost with an actual cost if the production level upon which the budgeted cost was based is not achieved.

The fixed overhead expenditure variance in the statement above also differs from the fixed overhead variance reported in the absorption costing statement. This is because the absorption costing statement compares overhead absorbed whereas the marginal costing statement compares overhead expenditure.

(v) There are other reasons why the reconciliation statement provides improved management information. (**Note.** Only ONE is actually required)

(1) It separates total variances into their components and so you will be able to determine whether, for example, the total material variance is the responsibility of the purchasing manager (price variance) or the production manager (usage variance).

(2) It avoids the use of under-or over-absorbed overhead, which is simply a bookkeeping exercise and does not reflect higher or lower cash spending.

(3) It allows management by exception. (Management by exception means concentrating on areas that require attention and ignoring areas which seem to be as expected.)

(4) The original statement conveys the wrong message (that the overall variance was favourable).

I hope this information has proved useful. If I can be of further assistance or you have any questions, please do not hesitate to contact me.

Task 5.7

			£
Budgeted/Standard cost for actual production			47,976
Variances	**Favourable £**	**Adverse £**	
Direct materials price		860	
Direct materials usage	426		
Direct labour rate	820		
Direct labour efficiency		1,530	
Fixed overhead expenditure		250	
Fixed overhead volume	560		
Total variance	1,806 (F)	2,640 (A)	834 (A)
Actual cost of actual production			48,810

Working:

Standard cost of actual production:

Budgeted cost per unit = £42,559/1,100 = £38.69 per unit

Budgeted cost of 1,240 units = £38.69 × 1,240 = £47,976

Fixed overhead expenditure variance – actual overheads larger than budgeted, therefore expenditure variance is adverse.

Direct materials usage variance – budgeted usage = 5,280/1,100 = 4.8 litres/unit

Actual usage = 5,800/1,240 = 4.68 litres/unit ie lower usage than budgeted so favourable.

Labour rate variance – budgeted rate = £23,375/2,750 = £8.50 per hour

Actual rate = £27,060/3,280 = £8.25 per hour ie lower rate than budgeted, so favourable.

Chapter 6

Task 6.1

Variance	Possible causes
Favourable materials price variance	• Negotiation of a better price from a supplier • Negotiation of a trade or bulk purchase discount from a supplier • Purchase of a lower grade of materials
Favourable materials usage variance	• Use of a higher grade of material which led to less wastage • Use of more skilled labour leading to less wastage than normal • New machinery which provides greater efficiency
Adverse labour rate variance	• Unexpected increase in labour costs • Use of a higher grade of labour than anticipated • Unexpectedly high levels of overtime
Adverse labour efficiency variance	• Use of a less skilled grade of labour • Use of a lower grade of material which takes longer to work on • More idle time than budgeted for • Poor supervision of the workforce • Problems with machinery

Task 6.2

Scenario	Possible effects
A business has had to use a less-skilled grade of labour in its production process	• Favourable labour rate variance • Adverse labour efficiency variance • Adverse materials usage variance
A factory had a machine breakdown which resulted in three days of production delays last month	• Adverse labour efficiency variance • Adverse idle time variance • Adverse fixed overhead expenditure variance (due to additional costs of mending the machine) • Adverse fixed overhead volume variance • Adverse fixed overhead efficiency variance • Adverse fixed overhead capacity variance

Task 6.3

The total materials price variance is £ 36,600 Adverse.

The non-controllable element of the materials price variance that has been caused by the price increase is £ 22,550 Adverse.

The controllable element of the materials price variance caused by other factors is £ 14,050 Adverse.

Workings

1 **Total materials price variance**

	£
Standard cost for actual quantity 45,100 × £8	360,800
Actual cost	397,400
	36,600 (A)

2   **Non-controllable variance caused by price increase**

	£
Standard cost for actual quantity 45,100 × £8	360,800
Adjusted cost for actual quantity 45,100 × £8.50	383,350
	22,550 (A)

3   **Controllable variance caused by other factors**

	£
Adjusted cost for actual quantity 45,100 × £8.50	383,350
Actual cost	397,400
	14,050 (A)

Task 6.4

The total materials price variance is   £   4,240   Adverse.

The non-controllable variance due to price increase is   £   5,300   Adverse.

The controllable variance due to other factors is   £   1,060   Favourable.

Workings

1   **Total materials price variance**

	£
Standard cost of actual quantity 10,600 × £6.50	68,900
Actual cost	73,140
	4,240 (A)

2   **Non-controllable variance due to price increase**

	£
Standard cost of actual quantity 10,600 × £6.50	68,900
Price adjusted cost of actual quantity 10,600 × £7.00	74,200
	5,300 (A)

3   **Controllable variance due to other factors**

	£
Price adjusted cost of actual quantity 10,600 × £7.00	74,200
Actual cost	73,140
	1,060 (F)

Task 6.5

The total materials price variance is £ 12,800 Favourable.

The non-controllable variance due to the season is £ 38,640 Favourable.

The controllable variance due to other factors is £ 25,840 Adverse.

Workings

1   **Total materials price variance**

	£
Standard cost of actual quantity 92,000 × £7.00	644,000
Actual cost	631,200
	12,800 (F)

2   **Non-controllable variance due to season**

	£
Standard cost of actual quantity 92,000 × £7.00	644,000
Seasonally adjusted price 92,000 × (£7.00 – £0.42)	605,360
	38,640 (F)

3   **Controllable variance due to other factors**

	£
Seasonally adjusted price 92,000 × (£7.00 – £0.42)	605,360
Actual cost	631,200
	25,840 (A)

Task 6.6

The total materials price variance is £ 25,380 Adverse.

The non-controllable variance caused by the seasonal price change is

£ 30,456 Adverse.

The controllable variance caused by other factors is £ 5,076 Favourable.

Workings

1 **Total materials cost variance**

	£
Standard cost of actual quantity 42,300 × £4.00	169,200
Actual cost	194,580
	25,380 (A)

2 **Non-controllable variance due to season**

	£
Standard cost of actual quantity 42,300 × £4.00	169,200
Seasonally adjusted cost 42,300 × (£4.00 + £0.72)	199,656
	30,456 (A)

3 **Controllable variance due to other factors**

	£
Seasonally adjusted cost 42,300 × (£4.00 + £0.72)	199,656
Actual cost	194,580
	5,076 (F)

Task 6.7

The total materials price variance is £ 26,000 Adverse.

The non-controllable variance caused by the index change is

£ 76,667 Adverse.

The controllable variance caused by other factors is £ 50,667 Favourable.

Workings

1 **Total materials cost variance**

	£
Standard cost of actual quantity 46,000 × £20	920,000
Actual cost	946,000
	26,000 (A)

2 **Non-controllable variance due to index change**

	£
Standard cost of actual quantity 46,000 × £20	920,000
Index adjusted cost 46,000 × £20 × 130/120	996,667
	76,667 (A)

3 **Controllable variance due to other factors**

	£
Index adjusted cost 46,000 × £20 × 130/120	996,667
Actual cost	946,000
	50,667 (F)

....

Task 6.8

(a) The part of the variance explained by the increase in the price index is

£ | 281,250 | .

	£
12,500 litres × £450 (original standard rate)	5,625,000
12,500 litres × £472.50 (£450 × 126.525/120.50)	5,906,250
	281,250 (A)

(b) The part of the variance not explained by the increase in the price index is

£ | 93,750 | .

£375,000 – £281,250 = £93,750

(c) The percentage increase in the index is [5] %.

(126.525 – 120.50)/120.50 = 0.05 (5%)

(d)

	September X3	December X3
Cost per kilogram of Z4QX(£)	2,136.62	2,543.84

Difference between April X3 and May X3 = £135.74

Difference between May X3 and June X3 = £135.74

September X3 cost = £1,729.40 (June X3) + (£135.74 × 3) = £2,136.62

December X3 cost = £2,136.62 (September X3) + (£135.74 × 3) = £2,543.84

(e) The forecast cost per kilogram, using the regression line, for September X3

is [£ | 118.85] .

June X3 is period 41. Therefore September X3 = period 44

y = 24.69 + 2.14x   where y = cost per kilogram   x = the period

y = 24.69 + (2.14 × 44)

y = 118.85

Task 6.9

(a) **(i)** **Actual litres of material used** = actual total cost of materials/actual cost per litre = £23,985/£58.50 = 410 litres

(ii) **Standard litres of material required for 40 barrels of X14** = standard litres per barrel × 40 = 10 litres × 40 = 400 litres

(iii) **Average actual labour rate per hour** = actual total cost of labour/actual number of hours = £2,788/328 hours = £8.50

(iv) **Standard labour hours required for 40 barrels of X14** = standard labour hours per barrel × 40 = 8 hours × 40 = 320 hours

(v) **Budgeted number of machine hours** = budgeted production × budgeted number of hours per barrel = 45 barrels × 16 = 720 hours

(vi) **Budgeted fixed overheads** = standard fixed overhead per barrel × budgeted production = £320 × 45 = £14,400

or = budgeted number of machine hours for processing department × standard rate per machine hour = 720 hours × £20 = £14,400

or = (budgeted machine hours for processing department/factory budgeted machine hours) × factory budgeted fixed overheads = (720 hours/1,152 hours) × £23,040 = £14,400)

(vii) Actual fixed overheads (for the processing department) = (budgeted machine hours for processing department/factory budgeted machine hours) × factory actual fixed overheads = (720 hours/1,152 hours) × £26,000 = £16,250

(viii) Standard machine hours for actual production = actual production output × standard machine hours per barrel = 40 barrels × 16 machine hours = 640 standard machine hours

(ix) Standard absorption cost of actual production = standard absorption cost per barrel × actual production = £984 × 40 barrels = £39,360

(x) Actual absorption cost of actual production = actual cost of material + labour + fixed overheads = £(23,985 + 2,788 + 16,250(a)(vii)) = £43,023

(b) **(i)** **Material price variance**

	£
410 litres (from (a)(i)) should have cost (× £60)	24,600
But did cost	23,985
	615 (F)

(ii) **Material usage variance**

40 barrels should have used (× 10 litres) (from (a)(ii))	400 litres
But did use (from (a)(i))	410 litres
Variance in litres	10 litres (A)
× standard cost per litre	× £60
	£600 (A)

(iii) Labour rate variance

	£
328 hours should have cost (× £8)	2,624
But did cost	2,788
	164 (A)

(iv) Labour efficiency variance

40 barrels should have taken (× 8 hours) (from (a)(iv))	320 hours
But did take	328 hours
Variance in hours	8 hours (A)
× standard cost per hour	× £8
	£64 (A)

(v) Fixed overhead expenditure variance

	£
Budgeted fixed overhead expenditure (from (a)(vi))	14,400
Actual fixed overhead expenditure (from (a)(vii))	16,250
	1,850 (A)

(vi) Fixed overhead volume variance

	£
Actual production at standard rate (40 barrels × £320)	12,800
Budgeted production at standard rate (45 barrels × £320)	14,400
	1,600 (A)

(c) **Reconciliation statement – five weeks ended 31 May 20X8**

	Favourable £	Adverse £	£
Standard absorption cost of actual production (from (a)(ix))			39,360
Variances			
Material price	615		
Material usage		600	
Labour rate		164	
Labour efficiency		64	
Fixed overhead expenditure		1,850	
Fixed overhead volume		1,600	
	615	4,278	3,663(A)
Actual absorption cost of actual production (from (a)(x))			43,023

(d)

MEMO

To:	Judith Green, production manager
From:	Accounting technician
Date:	7 August 20X5
Subject:	Croxton Ltd – analysis of variances for 5 weeks ended 31 May 20X8

Following our recent meeting, I set out below some issues to consider in relation to our discussions.

(i)   Revised standard material price per litre = £60 × 133/140 = £57

(ii) **Subdivision of material price variance**

	£	£
410 litres were expected to have cost (at the original standard of £60 per litre)	24,600	
but should then have been expected to have cost (at the revised standard of £57 per litre)	23,370	
Variance due to the change in the price index		1,230 (F)
410 litres should have cost, if the revised standard of £57 had been used	23,370	
but did cost	23,985	
Variance due to other reasons		615 (A)
Total material price variance		615 (F)

(iii) Reasons for the occurrence of the material price variance

A favourable material price variance of £615 was reported for the five weeks ended 31 May 20X8. The standard price used as the basis for this calculation was out of date, however, and was too high. If a more realistic standard had been used, the actual cost was in fact greater than the standard cost, not less than the standard cost. The purchasing department had therefore purchased material at a price greater than the realistic standard (although at a price lower than the out of date standard).

The purchasing department have therefore been inefficient, not efficient.

(iv) Implications of one scrapped barrel

(1) Material usage variance

The material usage variance shows that 10 litres more than standard were used. As the standard usage per barrel is 10 litres it is possible that the scrapped barrel is the reason for this adverse variance.

(2) Labour efficiency variance

The labour efficiency variance shows that eight hours more than standard were worked. As a standard eight hours should be worked per barrel it is possible that the scrapped barrel is the reason for this adverse variance.

(3) Labour rate variance

328 hours were actually worked during the five weeks. Overtime is paid on hours in excess of 320 hours, and hence an overtime premium of eight hours × £8 = £64 was paid in the period. Suppose the eight hours of overtime were worked because one barrel was scrapped (see (2) above). The total labour rate variance is £164 and so there is still £164 – £64 = £100 of the variance not explained by the scrapping of the barrel. This £100 would be due to other, unexplained reasons.

(v) Why the fixed overheads might not be controllable by the processing department

(1) The apportionment of both budgeted and fixed overheads to the department is done on the arbitrary basis of budgeted machine hours. Budgeted machine hours are determined by budgeted production volume, which is outside the control of the processing department.

(2) The actual overheads apportioned to the processing department are a share of total fixed overheads. The processing department is unable to control the fixed overheads incurred in other parts of Croxton Ltd, however.

Note. Only one reason was required for (v).

Task 6.10

(a) **(i)** **(1)** Actual number of meals served $=$ 4 meals × 7 days × 648 guests

$=$ 18,144 meals

(2) Standard number of meals for actual number of guests $=$ 3 meals × 7 days × 648 guests

$=$ 13,608 meals

(3) Actual hourly rate of pay $=$ £5,280/1,200 hours

$=$ £4.40 per hour

(4) Standard hours allowed for actual number of guests $=$ (648 guests × 3 meals × 7 days) /12 meals per hour

$=$ 1,134 hours

(5) Standard fixed overhead per guest $=$ budgeted overheads/budgeted number of guests

$=$ £38,340/540 = £71 per guest

(6) Total standard cost for actual number of guests

	£
Meal costs (13,608 meals × £3 per meal)	40,824
Catering staff costs (1,134 hours × £4 per hour)	4,536
Fixed overhead costs (648 × £71 per guest)	46,008
Total standard cost	91,368

(ii) **(1)**

	£
18,144 meals should cost (× £3)	54,432
but did cost	49,896
Material price variance for meals served	4,536 (F)

(2)

648 guests should have used ((a)(i)(2))	13,608 meals
but did use ((a)(i)(1))	18,144 meals
Usage variance in meals	4,536 meals (A)
× standard cost per meal	× £3
Material usage variance for meals served	£13,608 (A)

(3)

	£
1,200 hrs worked should have cost (× £4/hr)	4,800
but did cost	5,280
Labour rate variance for catering staff	480 (A)

(4)

Meals for 648 guests should have taken ((a)(i)(4))	1,134 hours
but did take	1,200 hours
Labour efficiency variance in hours	66 hours (A)
× standard rate per hour	× £4
Labour efficiency variance for catering staff	£264 (A)

(5)

	£
Budgeted fixed overhead expenditure	38,340
Actual fixed overhead expenditure	37,800
Fixed overhead expenditure variance	540 (F)

(6)

Actual number of guests	648
Budgeted number of guests	540
Volume variance – number of guests	108
× standard fixed overhead per guest ((a)(i)(5))	× £71
Fixed overhead volume variance	£7,668 (F)

(iii) **Bare Foot Hotel complex**

Standard cost reconciliation for seven days ended 27 November 20X8

Budgeted number of guests   540

Actual number of guests   648

	£		£	
Standard cost for 648 guests ((a)(i)(6))			91,368	
Cost variances				
Material price variance ((a)(ii)(1))	4,536	(F)		
Material usage variance ((a)(ii)(2))	13,608	(A)		
			9,072	(A)
Catering labour rate variance ((a)(ii)(3))	480	(A)		
Catering labour efficiency variance ((a)(ii)(4))	264	(A)		
			744	(A)
Fixed overhead expenditure variance ((a)(ii)(5))	540	(F)		
Fixed overhead volume variance ((a)(ii)(6))	7,668	(F)		
			8,208	(F)
Actual cost for 648 guests			92,976	

Note. (A) denotes adverse variance, (F) denotes favourable variance.

Task 6.11

Total direct material variance

The total direct material variance simply compares the **flexed budget** for materials with the actual cost incurred. The flexed budget is the total budgeted cost of materials for the actual production; 21,000 units in this example. It is incorrect to calculate the variance as £74,500 adverse by comparing the actual cost of £954,500 with the budgeted cost of £880,000.

The flexing of the budget calculates the **quantity of materials** which are expected to be used to produce the **actual production**. Therefore, the expected usage of materials to produce 21,000 units is £924,000 (if 80,000 kgs costing £880,000 is required to make 20,000 units then it follows, assuming that the material cost and quantity is perfectly variable, that to make 21,000 units requires 84,000 kilograms at a cost of £11 per kilogram (£880,000/80,000)).

This flexed budget can now be **compared with the actual** costs to produce the total material variance of £30,500. This variance is adverse because the **actual cost was greater than the flexed budgeted cost**.

This total variance can now be split into two elements:

- The variance due to the price being different to that which was expected. The material price variance.

- The variance due to the quantity of material used per unit of production being different to that which was expected. The material usage variance.

The expected (standard or budgeted or planned) price is £11 per kilogram (£880,000/80,000) and therefore the expected cost of 83,000 kilograms must be 83,000 kilograms at £11 per kilogram. This is £913,000.

The price variance can now be calculated by taking the actual cost (price paid) for the 83,000 kilograms and comparing this to the expected cost. This results in £913,000, compared to £954,500: a variance of £41,500. This variance is adverse because the **actual cost is greater than the expected cost**.

The material usage variance is calculated by taking the quantity of materials which would be expected to be used to produce the actual volume of production. In this case 21,000 units were produced and the expected quantity of materials for each unit is 4 kilograms (80,000 kilograms/20,000 units). Therefore, to produce 21,000 units requires 84,000 kilograms of material. Compare this to the actual quantity used of 83,000 kilograms produces a variance of 1,000 kilograms. This is favourable and needs to be **valued at the expected cost** of £11 per kilogram.

The usage variance is always **valued at the standard cost** (expected/planned or budgeted) because the price variance has already been isolated. If both variances have been calculated correctly they should reconcile back to the total materials variance. In this example, the price of £41,500 adverse less £11,000 favourable is reconciled to the total variance of £30,500.

....

Task 6.12

(a) **(i)** Standard price of materials per kg = $\dfrac{\text{Budgeted total materials cost}}{\text{Budgeted total materials usage in kg}}$

$$= \frac{£224,000}{56,000}$$

$$= £4 \text{ per kg}$$

(ii) Standard usage of materials per meal = $\dfrac{\text{Budgeted total materials usage in kg}}{\text{Production (meals)}}$

$$= \frac{56,000}{112,000}$$

$$= 0.5 \text{ kg}$$

(iii) Standard labour rate per hour $= \dfrac{\text{Budgeted total labour cost}}{\text{Budgeted total labour hours}}$

$$= \frac{£252,000}{28,000}$$

$$= £9 \text{ per hour}$$

(iv) Standard labour hours per meal $= \dfrac{\text{Budgeted total labour hours}}{\text{Production (meals)}}$

$$= \frac{28,000}{112,000}$$

$$= 0.25 \text{ hours (or 15 minutes)}$$

(v) Budgeted overhead absorption rate per hour =
$\dfrac{\text{Budgeted total overhead cost}}{\text{Budgeted total labour hours}}$

$$= \frac{£84,000}{28,000}$$

$$= £3 \text{ per hour}$$

(vi) Overheads absorbed into actual production $= 27,930 \text{ hours} \times £3$
$= £83,790$

(vii) Total standard cost of actual production $= £560,000 \times \dfrac{117,600}{112,000}$

$$= £588,000$$

Alternatively:

	Standard cost per meal £
Direct material (0.5 kg × £4)	2.00
Direct labour (0.25 hours × £9)	2.25
Fixed overheads (0.25 hours × £3)	0.75
	5.00

Total standard cost of actual production = 117,600 meals × £5 per meal
= £588,000

(b) Variance calculations:

	£
(i) Direct material price variance	
61,740 kg should have cost (× £4)	246,960
But did cost	185,220
	61,740 (F)
(ii) Direct material usage variance	
117,600 meals should have used (× 0.5 kg)	58,800
But did use	61,740
Variance in kg	2,940
at standard cost (× £4)	× £4
	11,760 (A)
(iii) Direct labour rate variance	
27,930 hours should have cost (× £9)	251,370
But did cost	279,300
	27,930 (A)

	£
(iv) Direct labour efficiency variance	
117,600 meals should have taken (× 0.25 hrs)	29,400
But did take	27,930
Variance in hrs	1,470
at standard cost (× £9)	× £9
	13,230 (F)
(v) Fixed overhead expenditure variance	
Budgeted fixed overhead	84,000
Actual fixed overhead	82,000
	2,000 (F)
(vi) Fixed overhead volume variance	
Actual production volume at standard rate (117,600 × 0.25 × £3)	88,200
Budgeted production volume at standard rate (112,000 × 0.25 × £3)	84,000
	4,200 (F)

This is a favourable variance because a greater production volume has been achieved than was budgeted for.

(c)

REPORT

To: Managing Director
From: Accounting Technician
Subject: Reasons for the variances
Date: 14 December 20X6

Having investigated the materials and labour variances calculated for November 20X6, I can suggest the following possible causes:

(i) Direct materials price variance £61,740 (F)

This variance resulted from the purchase of materials at £3 per kg rather than the standard cost of £4 per kg. This material was cheaper and possibly of a lower quality.

(ii) Direct material usage variance £11,760 (A)

The actual usage was worse than expected, and this could have been a consequence of buying inferior material.

(iii) Direct labour rate variance £27,930 (A)

Direct workers were actually paid at £10 per hour, whilst we had only budgeted for a rate of £9 per hour. It is possible that the workers used were more skilled than we planned for.

(iv) Direct labour efficiency variance £13,230 (F)

Actual production required fewer hours than were expected which is consistent with using more highly-skilled staff.

Note. There is more than one possible reason for each of the above variances, and marks would have been awarded for any reasonable suggestions.

Task 6.13

REPORT

To: Managing Director
From: Accountant
Date: xx.xx.xx
Subject: Reasons for variances

(a) Possible reasons for the variances:

Direct materials (carrots) price variance

The price variance for the carrots is £1,750 adverse. Soupzz Ltd is unable to control the price that it pays for its carrots as this is in part due to the weather. As there was bad flooding Soupzz had to find a supplier further away which appears to have pushed up the price resulting in an adverse variance.

Direct materials (carrots) usage variance

The usage variance for the carrots is £760 favourable. Due to the flooding, the regular suppliers were unable to provide the carrots demanded and as a result Soupzz Ltd had to look for alternative suppliers. They found suppliers who were able to provide a sweeter type of carrot, which resulted in less usage to obtain a similar soup taste and a favourable variance.

As a result of the change to sweeter carrots, fewer carrots were used in the production process. It would be useful to understand whether this had an impact on the taste of the soup to the consumer.

Direct materials (potatoes) price variance

The price variance for the potatoes is £450 favourable. There was a change in the general level of demand for potatoes which led to a reduction in price by the supplier. This had a positive impact for Soupzz and lowered the price they paid for the potatoes required.

Direct materials (potatoes) usage variance

The potatoes usage variance is £1,700 adverse. There was no change in the quality of the potatoes but the increase in usage of potatoes is due to the change in the sweetness of the carrots.

(b) During the machine downtime some of the labour staff had nothing to do. They have therefore been paid for more hours than they actually worked. This results in an idle time variance. As there was no idle time expected, this is an adverse idle time variance. The variance is the number of hours of idle time multiplied by the standard rate per hour.

Chapter 7

Task 7.1

Organisation	Possible productivity measures
Taxi firm	• Number of fares per shift • Number of miles per shift
Hospital	• Out-patients seen per day
Motorbike courier service	• Miles per week • Number of packages per day
Firm of accountants	• Chargeable hours as a percentage of total hours
Retail store	• Sales per employee • Sales per square foot of shop floor
Maker of hand-made pottery	• Number of pots thrown per day • Number of pots painted per day

Task 7.2

The total value added is **£** 394,200 .

The value added per employee is **£** 26,280 .

Working:

	£
Sales	1,447,600
Less: Cost of materials	(736,500)
Cost of services	(316,900)
Total value added	394,200
Value added per employee	394,200/15
	26,280

Task 7.3

(a)

	Calculation	Explanation
Efficiency ratio	92.61%	As the efficiency ratio is less than 100% this indicates that the workforce have not worked as efficiently as was anticipated. The actual hours worked are more than the standard hours for that level of production.
Capacity ratio	102.22%	The capacity ratio indicates whether as many hours have been worked as were budgeted for. In this instance the capacity ratio is greater than 100% meaning that the number of hours worked was more than those budgeted for.
Production volume ratio	94.67%	The production volume ratio is an indicator of how the volume of actual production compares to the budgeted level of output. In this instance as the production volume ratio is below 100% this indicates that the actual level of output was below the budgeted level.

Workings

(1) Efficiency ratio $= \dfrac{\text{Standard hours for actual production}}{\text{Actual hours worked}} \times 100$

$= \dfrac{14,200 \times 3}{46,000} \times 100$

$= 92.61\%$

(2) Capacity ratio $= \dfrac{\text{Actual hours worked}}{\text{Budgeted hours}} \times 100$

$= \dfrac{46,000}{15,000 \times 3} \times 100$

$= 102.22\%$

(3) Production volume ratio $= \dfrac{\text{Actual output}}{\text{Budgeted output}} \times 100$

$= \dfrac{14,200}{15,000} \times 100$

$= 94.67\%$

(b) Hours worked @ 95% efficiency $= \dfrac{14{,}200 \times 3}{0.95}$

$= 44{,}842$

Hours saved $(46{,}000 - 44{,}842)$ $= 1{,}158$ hours

....

Task 7.4

(a)

To: Finance Director
Subject: Differences in key performance indicators
From: Accounting Technician
Date: 18 June 20X7

(i) Gross profit margin

The gross profit margin for scenario 1 is 35% but falls to 10% for scenario 2. There are two causes for this difference. The selling price has been reduced by 50% (from £10 to £5) which will have reduced the margin. The reduction in the selling price has, however, increased the volume produced and sold which has reduced the fixed overhead per unit which will have increased the margin. However, the effect of the decreased selling price in reducing the margin has outweighed the beneficial effect of the fixed overheads.

(ii) Operating profit margin

The operating profit margin for scenario 1 is 20.5% and this falls to a loss under scenario 2. The reduction in gross profit margin has fed down to the operating profit margin and the selling and distribution costs have increased due to the higher sales volume.

(iii) Direct materials

The direct materials cost as a percentage of turnover has increased from 25% under scenario 1 to 50% under scenario 2. This difference is caused by the 50% reduction in the selling price. Every unit that is sold under the two scenarios has the same direct material cost (£2.50) but the selling price in scenario 2 is only £5 giving a percentage material cost of 50%, whereas the selling price in scenario 1 is £10 giving a percentage material cost of 25%.

(b)

	%
Gross profit margin £ $\left(\dfrac{540,000}{1,800,000}\right) \times 100$	30.00
Operating profit margin £ $\left(\dfrac{318,000}{1,800,000}\right) \times 100$	17.67
Return on net assets £ $\left(\dfrac{318,000}{1,043,000}\right) \times 100$	30.49

(c)

To: Financial Director
Subject: Differences in key performance indicators
From: Accounting Technician
Date: 18 June 20X7

(i) Gross profit margin

The revised gross profit has increased to 30%. The increase in the gross profit is caused by the reduction in the cost of raw materials per unit.

However, although the reduction in cost per unit increases the gross profit of scenario 2, it is still below the gross profit of scenario 1 because the effect of scenario 2's lower selling price outweighs the advantages of its lower raw materials and fixed cost absorption rate.

(ii) Operating profit margin

The revised operating profit for scenario 2 has increased to £318,000 from a loss. The operating profit margin is now improved to 18% which is fed through from the gross margin but this is still less than the 20.5% for scenario 1.

(iii) Return on net assets

The revised return on net assets for scenario 2 is 30.5% compared to 25% for scenario 1. The operating profit and net assets have been recalculated, thus giving us a revised figure of 30.5% for scenario 2. The return on net assets has increased by 5.5% due to an increase in operating profit. However, the net assets only increase by a modest amount in scenario 2, which suggests a more efficient use of resources than in scenario 1.

229

Recommendations

Based purely on the above three indicators, the decision should be to set the price at £5 as per scenario 2 because the higher return on net assets indicates that the return on investment is (pound for pound) better in scenario 2 and therefore will increase shareholder value. The fact that scenario 1 still has better gross and operating margins is not decisive. These margins do indicate that there are better operating efficiencies in scenario 1 compared to scenario 2. However, the fact that the revised figures for scenario 2 show that it has a significantly larger operating profit than scenario 1 with net assets for the two scenarios being almost the same causes the return on investment in scenario 2 to be better.

Task 7.5

(a)

	July	Aug	Sept	Oct	Nov	Dec
Gross profit margin	34%	34%	34%	32%	31%	31%
Operating profit margin	12%	12%	12%	11%	10%	9%
% of expenses to sales	22%	22%	22%	21%	21%	22%
Return on capital employed (W1)	15.2%	14.6%	13.1%	11.6%	10.9%	10.0%
Asset turnover (W2)	1.3	1.2	1.09	1.1	1.1	1.1

(b) Sales revenue decreased from July to September and then increased significantly until the end of the year. However the increase in sales has been at the cost of the gross profit margin which has decreased from 34% to 31%. Although the expenses to sales percentage has remained reasonably constant over the period, the operating profit margin has fallen due to the decrease in gross profit margin.

Return on capital employed fell dramatically in the first four months of the period although this was due to a significant decrease in asset turnover in that period more than a decline in profitability. The fall in return on capital employed continues in the last three months of the year due to the fall in operating profit margin; however the drop in return is not as bad as it might have been, as the asset turnover is again improving.

Workings

1 **Return on capital employed (ROCE)**

Here, return on capital employed is calculated as:

$$ROCE = \frac{Profit\ before\ interest}{Capital\ employed} = \frac{(550 - 374 - 116)}{468 + 50}$$

(shareholders funds + loan)

= 11.6% for October, etc

Alternatively, it may be computed as a return on net assets:

$$RONA = \frac{Profit\ after\ interest}{Shareholders'\ funds} = \frac{(550 - 374 - 116 - 3)}{468}$$

= 12.2% for October, etc

2 **Asset turnover**

To be consistent with the ROCE definition used, asset turnover has been calculated as:

$$Asset\ turnover = \frac{Revenue}{Total\ capital\ employed} = \frac{550}{468 + 50}$$

(shareholders' funds + loan)

= 1.06 for October, etc

Task 7.6

(a)

	North	**South**	**Central**
Gross profit margin	32.0%	30.0%	35.0%
Operating profit margin	18.0%	11.1%	13.4%
Return on capital employed	16.0%	9.0%	14.0%
Asset turnover	0.9	0.8	1.0
Inventory holding in months	0.7 months	1.1 months	1.0 months
Receivables' collection period in months	1.4 months	2.3 months	1.6 months
Payables' payment period in months	2.1 months	1.3 months	1.9 months

	North	South	Central
Units per square metre of floor area	34.0 units	25.5 units	29.3 units
Units produced per employee	944.4 units	850.0 units	820.0 units
Units produced per hour	2.0 units	1.8 units	1.8 units

(b) In terms of profitability North is clearly the most profitable with the highest operating profit margin and return on capital employed. However Central has a higher gross profit margin which may be due to production of a different product to North or due to higher local selling prices or lower purchasing prices for Central. Although Central's operating profit margin is significantly lower than North's its return on capital employed is not so different due to a higher asset turnover in Central. South seems to have profitability problems with gross and operating profit margins, asset turnover and return on capital employed significantly lower than those of the other two divisions.

North again appears to have the best working capital control with the lowest inventory holding and receivables' collection period and the longest payables' payment period. Central's working capital control appears to be adequate but again there are questions to be asked at South with a relatively long receivables' collection period and a month shorter payables' payment period.

Finally, whichever way productivity is measured, the productivity at North is significantly greater than at either of the other two divisions. Central makes the same number of units per hour as South but less per employee, indicating that there could be room for improvement in employee productivity at Central.

Workings

	North £	South £	Central £
Statement of profit or loss (Income statement)			
Revenue	870,000	560,000	640,000
COS: Opening inventory	34,000	41,000	34,000
Purchases	590,000	380,000	420,000
Closing inventory	(32,000)	(29,000)	(38,000)
	592,000	392,000	416,000
Gross profit	278,000	168,000	224,000

	North £	South £	Central £
Expenses	(121,000)	(106,000)	(138,000)
Operating profit	157,000	62,000	86,000
Statement of financial position			
Receivables	100,100	107,300	87,600
Payables	(103,400)	(42,600)	(66,700)
Other net assets	983,300	625,300	594,100
Capital	980,000	690,000	615,000

	North	South	Central
Gross profit margin	278/870	168/560	224/640
Operating profit margin	157/870	62/560	86/640
Return on capital employed	157/980	62/690	86/615
Asset turnover	870/980	560/690	640/615
Inventory holding in months (using average inventory)	33/592 × 12	35/392 × 12	36/416 × 12
Receivables' collection period in months	100.1/870 × 12	107.3/560 × 12	87.6/640 × 12
Payables' payment period in months	103.4/592 × 12	42.6/392 × 12	66.7/416 × 12
Units per square metre	17,000/500	10,200/400	12,300/420
Units per employee	17,000/18	10,200/12	12,300/15
Units per hour	17,000/8,500	10,200/5,800	12,300/7,000

Task 7.7

(a) Gross profit
= 380,000 × 0.48
= £182,400

(b) Sales
= £425,000/0.34
= £1,250,000

(c) Gross profit
= £85,000 × 0.40
= £34,000

Operating profit
= £85,000 × 0.115
= £9,775

Expenses
= £34,000 – £9,775
= £24,225

(d) Capital employed
= £100,000/0.116
= £862,069

(e) Asset turnover
= 0.10/0.08
= 1.25

(f) Average inventory
= (£158,000 + £182,000)/2
= £170,000

Cost of sales
= £158,000 + £560,000 – £182,000
= £536,000

Inventory turnover
= £536,000/£170,000
= 3.2 times

(g) Sales
= £96,000/48 × 365
= £730,000

Task 7.8

(a)

	Y/e 31 Dec 20X8	Y/e 31 Dec 20X7
Gross profit margin	45.3%	42.4%
Operating profit margin (Operating profit/Revenue)	18.3%	17.0%
Return on capital employed (Operating profit/ Share capital + Retained earnings + Loan)	14.7%	13.9%
Asset turnover	0.80	0.82
Non-current asset turnover	0.85	0.89
Current ratio	1.75	2.30
Quick ratio	1.2	1.6
Receivables' collection period	40 days	44 days
Inventory holding	31 days	36 days
Payables' payment period	61 days	51 days
Interest cover	11.0	9.6
Gearing ratio (Total debt/Share capital + Retained earnings)	25.0%	27.8%

(b) Return on capital employed has increased over the two-year period and this is solely due to increased profitability as both the asset turnover and non-current asset turnover have decreased over the period. There has been a significant increase in gross profit margin in 20X8 and, although operating profit margin has also increased, it has not done so at the rate of the gross profit margin, indicating that expenses are in fact increasing at a faster rate than sales. This may be due to a large advertising campaign which has increased costs but allowed the gross profit margin to increase or some similar reason.

As well as an increase in sales and profitability there also appears to be general improvement in the working capital management. Both the current and quick ratios have fallen but are still at acceptable levels. The receivables' collection period and inventory holding period have both been reduced by a few days and in combination with the increase in the

payables' payment period by 10 days this will have a significant positive effect on the cash flows of the business.

The level of gearing does not appear to be a problem, as the gearing ratios are quite low and the interest cover is quite high.

<hr />

Task 7.9

(a)

To: Angela Wade
From: A Technician
Date: xx.xx.xx
Subject: West Ltd and East Ltd – Performance Report

(i) **Return on net assets (RONA)**

The RONA is a key financial ratio which shows the amount of profit which has been made in relation to the amount of resources invested. It also gives some idea of how efficiently the company has been operating.

$$RONA = \frac{Operating\,profit}{Net\,assets}$$

$$RONA\,(West\,Ltd) = \frac{3,068}{15,340} = 0.2 \times 100\% = 20\%$$

$$RONA\,(East\,Ltd) = \frac{2,795}{6,500} = 0.43 \times 100\% = 43\%$$

(ii) **Net asset turnover**

The net asset turnover is one of the main ratios for the statement of financial position, and is a measure of how well the assets of a business are being used to generate sales.

$$Asset\,turnover = \frac{Net\,revenue}{Net\,assets}$$

$$Asset\,turnover\,(West\,Ltd) = \frac{17,910}{15,340} = 1.17\,times$$

$$Asset\,turnover\,(East\,Ltd) = \frac{17,424}{6,500} = 2.68\,times$$

(iii) **Operating profit margin**

The operating profit margin ratio is a measure of overall profitability and it provides a measure of performance for management. Unsatisfactory operating profit margins are investigated by management, and are generally followed by control action. Increasing selling prices and reducing costs will have a direct effect on this ratio.

$$\text{Operating profit margin} = \frac{\text{Operating profit}}{\text{Net revenue}}$$

$$\text{Operating profit margin (West Ltd)} = \frac{3,068}{17,910} = 0.171 \times 100\% = 17.1\%$$

$$\text{Operating profit margin (East Ltd)} = \frac{2,795}{17,424} = 0.16 \times 100\% = 16.0\%$$

(b) **Measure of customer service: faulty sales**

The percentage of faulty sales as a measure of the level of customer service is calculated as:

$$\frac{\text{Returns}}{\text{Gross sales}}$$

$$\text{West Ltd} = \frac{100}{20,000} = 0.005 \times 100\% = 0.5\%$$

$$\text{East Ltd} = \frac{220}{22,000} = 0.01 \times 100\% = 1.0\%$$

(c) **Further measure of customer service**

Another possible measure of the level of customer service which could be derived from the accounting data is the number of days between order and delivery of goods.

This can be calculated as follows.

$$\frac{\text{Time between}}{\text{order and delivery}} = \frac{\text{Orders received in year} - \text{net sales ('000 litres)}}{\text{Net sales ('000 litres)}} \times 365 \text{ days}$$

$$\text{West Ltd} = \frac{20,173 - 19,900}{19,900} \times 365 \text{ days} = 5 \text{ days}$$

$$\text{East Ltd} = \frac{22,854 - 21,780}{21,780} \times 365 \text{ days} = 18 \text{ days}$$

The amount of money which the subsidiaries invest in research and development, and training could also provide a measure of customer service.

(d) **Limitations of financial ratios**

Financial ratios as a measure of performance are only concerned with the data recorded in the accounts. For example, East Ltd appears to be a much more efficient company than West Ltd based on its RONA and net asset turnover ratios. However, when calculations are made to measure customer service, West Ltd has far fewer days between order and delivery of goods, and half as many faulty sales (as a percentage of gross sales).

The financial ratios also treat research and development, and training costs as expenses which are written off to the statement of profit or loss (income statement). These expenses are likely to have an impact on the future profitability of the company, and are more of an investment than expense.

Both West Ltd and East Ltd use plant of similar size and technology. There is however, a large difference in the net book values of the plant, and hence a large difference in the net assets of each company.

East Ltd purchased its plant before West Ltd, and has a lower cost, and a higher depreciation to date than West Ltd. These differences arise mainly due to the fact that the accounts are prepared using historic cost accounting. The fact that East Ltd's net assets are so much lower than those of West Ltd, means that the RONA of East Ltd will be much higher than that of West Ltd.

Task 7.10

(a)

Performance indicator	Workings	
Return on net assets	(Operating profit/Net assets) × 100% (975,000/4,875,000) × 100%	20%
Net asset turnover	Revenue/Net assets 3,900,000/4,875,000	0.8
Operating profit margin	(Operating profit/Revenue) × 100% (975,000/3,900,000) × 100%	25%

Performance indicator	Workings	
Average age of receivables in months	(Receivables/Revenue) × 12 (325,000/3,900,000) × 12	1 month
Average age of finished inventory in months	(Average finished goods inventory/Cost of sales) × 12 (½ × (140,000 + 50,000)/840,000) × 12	1.4 months

(b)

Briefing notes on the usefulness of performance indicators

Prepared for: Angela Frear
Prepared by: Financial Analyst
Dated: xx.xx.xx

(i) Return on net assets

The return on net assets can be misleading:

(1)   Profits should be related to average capital employed but we compute the ratio using year-end assets. Using year-end figures can distort trends and comparisons. If a new investment is undertaken near to a year end and financed, for example, by an issue of shares, the capital employed will rise by the finance raised but profits will only have a month or two of the new investment's contribution.

(2)   The RONA would be higher if costs such as marketing, research and development and training were not treated as revenue expenditure but were viewed as investment for the future and were capitalised.

(ii) Operating profit margin

The operating profit margin can be manipulated in a number of ways. The following activities would result in short-term improvements in the margin, but probably at the expense of the organisation's long-term viability:

(1)   Reducing expenditure on discretionary cost items such as research and development.

(2)   Depreciating assets over a longer period of time, so that the depreciation charge is less.

(3)   Choosing an alternative inventory valuation method to increase the value of closing inventory.

BPP
LEARNING MEDIA

Average delay in fulfilling orders

	£
Orders during the year	4,550,000
Revenue during the year	3,900,000
Unfulfilled orders	650,000

Average delay = (£650,000/£3,900,000) × 12 months = 2 months

(iv) Measures of customer satisfaction

As well as the delay in fulfilling orders, other measures of customer satisfaction include the following:

- Repeat business ((£3,120,000/£3,900,000) × 100% = 80%)

- Cost of customer support per £ of revenue (£400,000/£3,900,000 = 10p)

- Cost of customer support per customer (information not available)

(v) Measuring performance from an internal perspective

A number of indicators may help to measure performance from an internal perspective:

- Training costs as a percentage of production costs ((£140,000/£930,000) × 100% = 15.05%)

- Reworked faulty production as a percentage of total production ((£37,200/£930,000) × 100% = 4%)

- Returns as a percentage of sales ((£100,000/£4m) × 100% = 2.5%)

The first indicator should be relatively high, the second and third as low as possible.

> **(vi) Measuring the innovation and learning perspective**
>
> The innovation and learning perspective could be measured with one of the following indicators:
>
> - Revenue from new products as a percentage of total revenue (($£1.56m/£3.9m) \times 100\% = 40\%$)
>
> - Research and development expenditure as a percentage of cost of production (($£750,000/£930,000) \times 100\% = 81\%$)
>
> - Research and development expenditure as a percentage of revenue (($£750,000/£3.9m) \times 100\% = 19.2\%$)
>
> **Note.** A fuller answer has been given here than was required in the task for assessment purposes, where in most cases only ONE point was required.

Task 7.11

(a) **(i)** Gross profit margin $= \dfrac{£221,760}{£633,600} \times 100\% = 35\%$

(ii) Operating profit margin $= \dfrac{£76,032}{£633,600} \times 100\% = 12\%$

(iii) Return on capital employed $= \dfrac{£76,032}{£95,040} \times 100\% = 80\%$

(iv) Asset turnover $= \dfrac{£633,600}{£95,040} = 6.7 \text{ times}$

(v) No. of passengers in the year $= \dfrac{\text{Revenue (turnover)}}{\text{Fare per passenger}} = \dfrac{£633,600}{£1}$

$= 633,600 \text{ passengers}$

(vi) Total cost per mile $= \dfrac{£633,600 - £76,032}{356,400} = £1.56$

(vii) No. of journeys in the year $= \dfrac{356,400}{18 \text{ miles per journey}} = 19,800 \text{ journeys}$

No. of journeys per day $= \dfrac{19,800}{360} = 55 \text{ journeys}$

(viii) Maintenance cost per mile $= \dfrac{£28,512}{356,400} = £0.08$

(ix) Passengers per day $= \dfrac{633,600 \text{ (from (v))}}{360} = 1,760$ passengers

(x) Passengers per journey $= \dfrac{1,760 \text{ (from (ix))}}{55 \text{ (from (vii))}} = 32$ passengers

(xi) Number of drivers $= \dfrac{\text{Wages paid}}{\text{Wages per driver}} = \dfrac{£142,000}{£14,200} = 10$ drivers

(b)

MEMO

To: Chief executive
From: Management accountant
Date: xx.xx.xx
Subject: Performance of Travel Bus Ltd for the year to 30 November 20X8

This memo addresses a number of issues concerning the productivity and profitability of Travel Bus Ltd.

(i) Productivity and profitability

Productivity is the quantity of service produced (output) in relation to the resources put in (input). It measures how efficiently resources are being used.

An increase in productivity does not always lead to increased profitability. For example the number of passengers carried per driver, a measure of productivity, could increase. The extra passengers may have been attracted by offering substantial fare reductions, however, and this could lead to reduced profitability.

Another example might be an increase in productivity in terms of the number of journeys per bus. This increase in 'output' arising from the increase in productivity may not be saleable: the buses may be running empty. The revenue gained might be less than the additional costs incurred, leading to reduced profitability.

(ii) Driver productivity

A possible measure of driver productivity is the number of miles per driver.

	20X7	20X8
Miles per driver	$\dfrac{324,000}{8} = 40,500$	$\dfrac{356,400}{10} = 35,640$

The number of miles per driver has decreased between 20X7 and 20X8 and so, in terms of this measure of productivity, the drivers' claim that their productivity has increased is incorrect.

Even if the productivity had increased, the drivers might still be unable to claim that this had resulted in improved profitability. As discussed above, the extra miles might have been travelled with too few fare-paying passengers, so profitability would not necessarily have improved.

(iii) Reason for improved profitability

A major reason for the improved profitability was the Council's decision not to charge for parking. This reduced the overall cost of using the service for passengers, and demand therefore increased considerably. Since many of the costs incurred by Travel Bus Ltd are fixed, costs did not increase at the same rate as revenue, and profitability improved.

(iv) Performance indicators to measure the satisfaction of passenger needs

(1) The satisfaction of passenger needs could be monitored by the number of passengers per journey.

	20X7	20X8
Number of passengers per journey	30	32

Depending on the size of the buses, passenger needs may have been less satisfied during 20X8 because of more crowding or the need to stand because no seats were available.

Another measure of the satisfaction of passenger needs is the number of journeys per day.

	20X7	20X8
Number of journeys per day	50	55

This increase probably led to reduced waiting times and so passenger needs may have been better satisfied in 20X8.

(2) A measure of the satisfaction of customer needs that cannot be derived from the existing data is cleanliness of the buses.

Monitoring the cleaning cost per day or per bus might give some indication of the effort put into keeping the buses clean.

Another measure of the satisfaction of customer needs is punctuality of the buses and their adherence to published timetables.

Monitoring the percentage of buses arriving and departing within five minutes of their published time would give an indication of performance in this area.

Note. Only one measure required by the task

(v) Monitoring the safety aspect of Travel Bus's operations

(1) The safety aspect of Travel Bus's operations could be monitored by the maintenance cost per mile.

	20X7	20X8
Maintenance cost per mile	£0.10	£0.08

This has reduced, which may indicate a reduction in attention to safety, especially as maintenance costs are likely to increase as buses become older. No new buses have been added to the fleet (cost value of buses has remained at £240,000); the buses are older and likely to require more maintenance.

On the other hand, some of this reduction in the cost per mile may have been caused by the spreading of the fixed element of maintenance costs over a higher number of miles in the year 20X8.

Another indicator of attention to the safety aspect might be the average age of the buses. The depreciation charge for the year 20X8 was £12,000 (£180,000 – £168,000). On a cost value of £240,000, assuming straight line depreciation and no residual value, this suggests a useful life of 20 years. Accumulated depreciation of £180,000 means that the buses were on average 15 years old by the end of 20X6, and thus nearing the end of their useful lives.

(2) A measure of the safety aspect that cannot be derived from the existing data is the number of accidents per year.

Another measure could be the percentage of maintenance cost that is incurred to prevent faults compared with the percentage incurred to correct faults. This would indicate whether faults were being prevented before they occurred, or whether maintenance was being carried out 'after the event', which could compromise safety.

Note. Only one measure required by the task.

Task 7.12

(a) Budgeted statements of profit or loss (income statements)

	Pickmaster £	Pickmaster 2 £
Revenue	1,125,000	1,125,000
Cost of sales		
Tea pickers	150,000	150,000
Tea processor operators (W)	48,000	4,800
Depreciation (W)	16,000	72,000
Seed and fertiliser costs	75,000	75,000
Total cost of sales	289,000	301,800
Gross profit	836,000	823,200
Administration costs	150,000	135,000
Distribution costs	350,000	350,000
Operating profit	336,000	338,200

Net assets at year end

	Pickmaster £	Pickmaster 2 £
Budgeted net assets	935,500	935,500
Operating profit	336,000	338,200
	1,271,500	1,273,700

Workings

	Pickmaster £	Pickmaster 2 £
Tea processor operators (10 × £6 × 100 × 8)	48,000	
(1 × £6 × 100 × 8)		4,800
Depreciation of tea machines (8 × £2,000)	16,000	
(8 × £9,000)		72,000

Note. The value of the new machines has not been included in the net asset figure as their purchase would have to be funded in some way ie bank loan, leasing, leading to an increase in liabilities which would cancel out the increase in asset values. This will not be an exact cancellation but we have no information about the method of funding.

(b)

	Pickmaster	Pickmaster 2
Gross profit margin	74.31%	73.17%
Operating profit margin	29.87%	30.06%
Return on net assets	26.43%	26.55%

Workings

		Pickmaster %	Pickmaster 2 %
1	**Gross profit margin**		
	$\dfrac{836,000}{1,125,000} \times 100$	74.31	
	$\dfrac{823,200}{1,125,000} \times 100$		73.17

		Pickmaster %	Pickmaster 2 %
2	**Operating profit margin**		
	$\dfrac{336,000}{1,125,000} \times 100$	29.87	
	$\dfrac{338,200}{1,125,000} \times 100$		30.06
3	**Return on net assets**		
	$\dfrac{336,000}{1,271,500} \times 100$	26.43	
	$\dfrac{338,200}{1,273,700} \times 100$		26.55

(c)

REPORT

To: Managing Director
From: Accounting technician
Date: December 20X7
Subject: Purchase of new machinery

I have been asked to write this report with regard to the decision as to whether to replace our current tea machines with eight new Pickmaster machines or Pickmaster 2 machines.

Performance indicators

(i) In terms of our profitability and return on net assets, there is little to be chosen between the two options. The Pickmaster machines give a slightly higher gross profit margin due to the much smaller depreciation charge, although costing more in terms of tea processor operators. However due to a reduction in administration costs if the Pickmaster 2 machines are purchased, then the gross profit and operating profit margins hardly differ under the two options. Equally the return on net assets under each of the two options is very similar.

Other considerations

(ii) Firstly we need to consider the funding of the purchase of these machines. If the Pickmaster machines are purchased then they will cost £160,000 (8 × £20,000) but if the Pickmaster 2 machines are purchased then these will cost £720,000 (8 × £90,000). These purchases will have to be funded in some way such as a bank loan or by purchasing them under lease finance. In either event if the Pickmaster 2 machines are purchased then this will significantly increase the gearing of the organisation and incur high service costs in the form of interest payments on a loan or finance charges on a lease.

The second consideration is the relative benefits and costs of the two machines. The advantage of the Pickmaster 2 is that only 1 operator per day is required rather than 10. However these operators are employed as and when needed on temporary contracts, therefore if the harvest was low less operatives could be employed. However the depreciation charges on the machines at £72,000 (8 × £9,000) for the Pickmaster 2 machines compared to £16,000 (8 × £2,000) for the Pickmaster machines are fixed costs that will be incurred whatever the level of revenue and harvest. Therefore, if there is a low harvest investment in the Pickmaster 2 machines will depress profit.

Note. A third consideration might be the expected residual value of each type of machine at the end of the 10-year period but only two further considerations were required for the task.

Conclusion

(iii) As the choice of machines has little effect on profit at the budgeted level but the Pickmaster 2 machines increase the risk of the operation, due to increased gearing and depreciation charges, then on balance purchase of the Pickmaster machines for £160,000 would be recommended.

Task 7.13

(a) **Performance indicators**

(i)

September	October	November
Profit margin		
$\dfrac{£148,687}{£690,000} \times 100$	$\dfrac{£154,125}{£697,200} \times 100$	$\dfrac{£125,480}{£672,000} \times 100$
= 21.55%	= 22.11%	= 18.67%

(ii) Direct material cost as a percentage of revenue

$$\frac{£185,000}{£690,000} \times 100 \qquad \frac{£185,100}{£697,200} \times 100 \qquad \frac{£185,220}{£672,000} \times 100$$

$$= 26.81\% \qquad\qquad = 26.55\% \qquad\qquad = 27.56\%$$

(iii) Direct labour cost as a percentage of revenue

$$\frac{£274,313}{£690,000} \times 100 \qquad \frac{£275,975}{£697,200} \times 100 \qquad \frac{£279,300}{£672,000} \times 100$$

$$= 39.76\% \qquad\qquad = 39.58\% \qquad\qquad = 41.56\%$$

(iv) Return on capital employed (ROCE)

$$\frac{£148,687}{£1,211,000} \times 100 \qquad \frac{£154,125}{£1,218,700} \times 100 \qquad \frac{£125,480}{£1,204,700} \times 100$$

$$= 12.28\% \qquad\qquad = 12.65\% \qquad\qquad = 10.42\%$$

Alternatively:

$$\frac{£148,687}{£2,011,000} \times 100 \qquad \frac{£154,125}{£2,018,700} \times 100 \qquad \frac{£125,480}{£2,004,700} \times 100$$

$$= 7.39\% \qquad\qquad = 7.63\% \qquad\qquad = 6.26\%$$

(v) Meals produced as a percentage of orders

$$\frac{115,500}{115,000} \qquad\qquad \frac{116,200}{117,000} \qquad\qquad \frac{117,600}{112,000}$$

$$= 100.43\% \qquad\qquad = 99.32\% \qquad\qquad = 105.00\%$$

(vi) Meals produced as a percentage of capacity

$$\frac{115,500}{125,000} \qquad\qquad \frac{116,200}{125,000} \qquad\qquad \frac{117,600}{125,000}$$

$$= 92.4\% \qquad\qquad = 92.96\% \qquad\qquad = 94.08\%$$

(b)

This report examines key areas of the performance of the catering division in November 20X6.

(i)   Overall, the division performed significantly worse in November compared with the previous two months. Profit margin fell by 13% from 21.55% in October to 18.67%, and ROCE fell by 15% from 12.28% to 10.42% in the same period.

(ii) The problem in the division arises from the difference between meals ordered and meals produced in November. 117,600 meals were produced, which was 5% greater than the number ordered of 112,000. As the meals are perishable, excess production one day cannot be used the next day, and so leads to wastage.

(iii) The excess production in November meant that materials and labour costs were increased without the costs being recovered in increased sales.

(iv) The division worked at 94.08% of capacity in the month. We would not expect full capacity at all times as work should only be done to fulfil orders placed.

(c) **(i)**

	Renting £	Purchasing £
Revenue (120,000 × £6)	720,000	720,000
Cost of sales		
Materials (120,000 × £2)	240,000	240,000
Labour (120,000 × £1.50)	180,000	180,000
Fixed overheads	82,000	82,000
Rent	50,000	
Depreciation (£3m – £900,000)/(12 × 10 months)		17,500
Total cost of sales	552,000	519,500
Profit	168,000	200,500
Net assets		
(£1,204,700 + £168,000)	1,372,700	
(£1,204,700 + £1m + £200,500)		2,405,200

(ii)

	Renting	Purchasing
Profit margin =	$\dfrac{£168,000}{£720,000} \times 100$	$\dfrac{£200,500}{£720,000} \times 100$
	= 23.33%	= 27.85%
ROCE =	$\dfrac{£168,000}{£1,372,700} \times 100$	$\dfrac{£200,500}{£2,405,200} \times 100$
	= 12.24%	= 8.34%

(iii) Renting the machine gives a higher ROCE than buying the machine because the higher profit earned with a bought machine is outweighed by the large increase in net assets. Therefore the machine should be rented rather than bought. However, the ROCE is not necessarily improved when compared with the figures for October to November 20X6, and further consideration should be given to whether the machine is obtained at all.

Task 7.14

(a) Sales price and sales volume

The sales price is higher for S1 which will improve the gross profit margin for S1. However, the sales volume is higher for S2, which will improve the gross profit margin for this product as there are fixed production costs that remain constant. This is because these costs will be spread over more units therefore increasing the gross profit per unit.

(b) Material cost

The material cost per unit is constant which therefore has no effect on the gross profit margin.

(c) Fixed production cost

The fixed production cost is constant which means that the increased volume will reduce the fixed cost per unit. This is because the fixed costs are being spread over more units. A lower fixed cost per unit will increase the gross profit margin for S2.

....

Task 7.15

(a)

	Scenario 1	Scenario 2
Return on net assets	11.96%	9.52%
Inventory holding period in days	50.00	45.29
Sales price per unit	£14.00	£12.00
Full production cost per unit	£9.00	£9.00

Workings

1 Return on net assets

Scenario 1 = £275,000/£2,298,400 × 100% = 11.96%
Scenario 2 = £200,000/£2,100,340 × 100% = 9.52%

2 Inventory holding period

Scenario 1 = £147,950/(£1,680,000 − £600,000) × 365 = 50.00 days
Scenario 2 = £167,500/(£1,800,000 − £450,000) × 365 = 45.29 days

3 Sales price per unit

Scenario 1 = £1,680,000/120,000 = £14.00
Scenario 2 = £1,800,000/150,000 = £12.00

4   Full production cost per unit

Scenario 1 = (£1,680,000 – £600,000)/120,000 = £9.00
Scenario 2 = (£1,800,000 – £450,000)/150,000 = £9.00

(b)

	Scenario 3
Net assets (£)	175,000
Return on net assets (%)	13
Profit margin (%)	14
Gearing (%)	32.75
Profit (to the nearest £)	22,750
Sales revenue (to the nearest £)	162,500

Working:

Profit (to the nearest £) = £175,000 × (13/100) = £22,750

Sales revenue (to the nearest £) = £22,750/(14/100) = £162,500

(c)

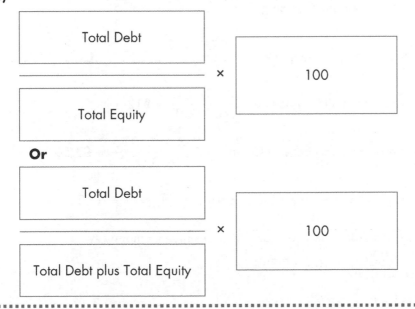

Total Debt / Total Equity × 100

Or

Total Debt / Total Debt plus Total Equity × 100

Task 7.16

(a)

	Company A	Company B
Selling price per unit (£)	42	35
Labour cost per unit (£)	18	12
Fixed production cost per unit (£)	3.50	3.00
Selling and distribution costs (as a % of revenue)	2.38	3.43
Gross profit margin (%)	32.14	40
Profit margin (%)	21.19	24
Return on net assets (%)	9	19.60

Workings

Selling price per unit Company A $\dfrac{37,800,000}{900,000} = £42$

Selling price per unit Company B $\dfrac{49,000,000}{1,400,000} = £35$

Labour cost per unit Company A $\dfrac{16,200,000}{900,000} = £18$

Labour cost per unit Company B $\dfrac{16,800,000}{1,400,000} = £12$

Fixed production cost per unit Company A $\dfrac{3,150,000}{900,000} = £3.50$

Fixed production cost per unit Company B $\dfrac{4,200,000}{1,400,000} = £3$

Selling and distribution costs as a % of revenue Company A
$\left(\dfrac{900,000}{37,800,000}\right) \times 100 = 2.38\%$

Selling and distribution costs as a % of revenue Company B
$\left(\dfrac{1,680,000}{49,000,000}\right) \times 100 = 3.43\%$

Gross profit margin % Company A $\left(\dfrac{12,150,000}{37,800,000}\right) \times 100 = 32.14\%$

Gross profit margin % Company B $\left(\dfrac{19,600,000}{49,000,000}\right) \times 100 = 40\%$

Profit margin % Company A $\left(\dfrac{8,010,000}{37,800,000}\right) \times 100 = 21.19\%$

Profit margin % Company B $\left(\dfrac{11,760,000}{49,000,000}\right) \times 100 = 24\%$

Return on net assets % Company A $\left(\dfrac{8,010,000}{89,000,000}\right) \times 100 = 9\%$

Return on net assets % Company B $\left(\dfrac{11,760,000}{60,000,000}\right) \times 100 = 19.6\%$

(b)

Ratio	Year 1 %	Year 2 %
Labour efficiency ratio	96.25	105.37

Working:

Year 1 $\left(\dfrac{(37,200 \times 0.8)}{30,920}\right) \times 100 = 96.25\%$

Year 2 $\left(\dfrac{(51,000 \times 0.8)}{38,720}\right) \times 100 = 105.37\%$

Task 7.17

	January	February	March
Productivity per labour hour	0.99 units	1.11 units	1.00 units
Efficiency ratio	108.78%	121.96%	110.47%
Capacity ratio	92.35%	86.69%	88.80%
Activity ratio	100.47%	105.73%	98.11%
Value added per employee	£6,613.00	£6,445.00	£5,784.00

Workings

		January	February	March
1	**Productivity per labour hour**	$\dfrac{8,540}{8,635}$	$\dfrac{8,670}{7,820}$	$\dfrac{9,320}{9,280}$
		0.99 units per hour	1.11 units per hour	1.00 unit per hour
2	**Efficiency ratio**	$\dfrac{8,540 \times 1.1}{8,635}$	$\dfrac{8,670 \times 1.1}{7,820}$	$\dfrac{9,320 \times 1.1}{9,280}$
		108.78%	121.96%	110.47%
3	**Capacity ratio**	$\dfrac{8,635}{8,500 \times 1.1}$	$\dfrac{7,820}{8,200 \times 1.1}$	$\dfrac{9,280}{9,500 \times 1.1}$
		92.35%	86.69%	88.80%
4	**Activity ratio**	$\dfrac{8,540}{8,500}$	$\dfrac{8,670}{8,200}$	$\dfrac{9,320}{9,500}$
		100.47%	105.73%	98.11%

		£	£	£
5	**Value added per employee**			
	Sales	916,000	923,000	965,000
	Production costs	(552,300)	(568,500)	(629,500)
	Value added	363,700	354,500	335,500
	Value added per employee	6,613	6,445	5,784

Task 7.18

(a)

Gross profit margin	30%
Operating profit margin	23%
Direct materials cost per unit	£3 per unit
Receivables' collection period in days	73 days

Workings

1   **Gross profit**

$$= \frac{£1,200,000}{£4,000,000} \times 100 = 30\%$$

2   **Operating profit margin**

$$= \frac{£905,000}{£4,000,000} \times 100 = 23\%$$

3   **Direct materials cost per unit**

$$= \frac{£1,500,000}{500,000} = £3 \text{ per unit}$$

4   **Receivables' collection period in days**

$$= \frac{£800,000}{£4,000,000} \times 365 = 73 \text{ days}$$

(b)

To:	Finance Director
Subject:	Key performance indicators
From:	Accounting Technician
Date:	26 October 20X2

(i)   Gross profit margin – selling price to achieve industry margin

The current gross profit margin is 30% but the industry margin is 35%. Therefore, for the same level of costs, the sales price would have to increase to £8.62 per unit.

(ii)   Operating profit margin – percentage reduction in administration costs

For an operating profit margin of 25% when the only cost/revenue that can change is administration costs, these would have to decrease by 45.24%

(iii)   Receivables' collection period – change to achieve industry average

Receivables would have to reduce by £87,671 to achieve the industry average of receivables' days of 65, for this level of revenue.

Workings

1 **Gross profit margin of 35%**

Cost of sales = £2,800,000

Revenue would have to be £2,800,000/65% = £4,307,692

Sales price per unit would have to be £4,307,692/500,000 = £8.62

2 **Operating profit margin of 25%**

Operating profit/revenue = 25%

Revenue would be unchanged, so operating profit would be 25% × £4,000,000 = £1,000,000 ie an increase of £95,000.

Therefore, fixed administration overheads would have to decrease by £95,000.

Percentage reduction in fixed administration overheads = £95,000/£210,000 = 45.24%

3 **Industry receivables' days are 65 days**

Revenue × 65/365 = receivables

£4,000,000 × 65/365 = £712,329

Reduction in receivables = £800,000 – £712,329 = £87,671

Chapter 8

Task 8.1

(a) The product lifecycle is generally thought to split naturally into five separate stages:

- Development
- Launch
- Growth
- Maturity
- Decline

During the development and launch stage of the product's life there are large outgoings in terms of development expenditure, non-current assets necessary for production, the building up of inventory levels and advertising and promotion expenses. It is likely that even after the launch sales will be quite low and the product will be making a loss at this stage.

If the launch of the product is successful then during the growth stage there will be fairly rapid increases in sales and a move to profitability as the costs of the earlier stages are covered. However, these sales increases are not likely to continue indefinitely.

In the maturity stage of the product demand for the product will probably start to slow down and become more constant. In many cases this is the stage where the product is modified or improved in order to sustain demand and this may then see a small surge in sales.

At some point in a product's life, unless it is a consumable item such as chocolate bars, the product will reach the end of its sales life, this is known as the decline stage. The market will have bought enough of the product and sales will decline. This is the point where the business should consider no longer producing the product.

(b) If the future demand for a product is to be forecast using time series analysis it is obviously important that the stage in the product lifecycle that has been reached is taken into account. For example, if the trend is based upon the growth stage whereas in fact the product is moving into the maturity stage then the trend would show an overly optimistic forecast for sales.

Task 8.2

The target cost of the new product is | £ | 40 | .

Working:

Target cost = Market price – Desired profit margin
= £50 – (£50 × 20%)
= £50 – £10
= £40

Task 8.3

The target cost per unit is | £ | 7.50 | .

Working:

Target cost = Price – Desired profit margin
= £25 – (£25 × 70%)
= £7.50 per unit

Sales price per unit = £250,000/10,000 = £25

Task 8.4

(a)

	Sales price £40	Sales price £50
The target total production cost per unit	£28	£35
The target fixed production cost per unit	£16	£22
The target fixed production cost	£8,000,000	£9,460,000

Workings

1 **Target total production cost per unit**

Sales price £40 = £40 × 70/100 = £28
Sales price £50 = £50 × 70/100 = £35

2 **Target fixed production cost per unit**

Sales price £40 = £28 – £12 = £16
Sales price £50 = £35 – £13 = £22

3 **Target fixed production cost**

Sales price £40 = £16 per unit × 500,000 = £8,000,000
Sales price £50 = £22 per unit × 430,000 = £9,460,000

(b) Alpha should set the price at ☐ £50 ☐ in order to achieve the target profit margin.

··

Task 8.5

(a) The profit achieved is | £ | 120,000 | .

(b) The profit achieved is | £ | 80,000 | .

(c) The profit achieved is | £ | 100,000 | .

(d) The sales price per unit will need to be | £ | 62.50 | to achieve a profit margin of 20%.

(e) The sales price to achieve a mark up of 30% is | £ | 104 | .

Workings

1 6,000 × £90 = £540,000. Less: 6,000 × £70 = £420,000. Profit £120,000

2 8,000 × £70 = £560,000. Less: 8,000 × £60 = £480,000. Profit £80,000

Note. The £60 cost per unit includes £30 fixed costs (£240,000/8,000).

3 6,000 × £70 = £420,000. Less: 6,000 × £70 = £420,000. Profit £0

Breakeven on the 6,000 units manufactured and sold at £70

Profit of £25 per unit on the units from overseas, 4,000 × £25 = £100,000

4 $\dfrac{£50}{(1-0.2)}$ = £62.50. Proof: £62.50 less £50 = £12.50

Check: Profit margin: $\left(\dfrac{12.50}{62.50}\right) \times 100 = 20\%$

5 £80/100 × 130 = £104

··

Chapter 9

Task 9.1

(a) The price of job HMG/012 based upon direct costs plus 50%

mark-up is   £ | 457,500 .

The price of job CFG/013 based upon direct costs plus 50%

mark-up is   £ | 279,000 .

	HMG/012 £	CFG/013 £
Equipment cost	175,000	120,000
Direct labour cost	130,000	66,000
Total direct cost	305,000	186,000
Mark up	50%	50%
Price	457,500	279,000

(b) Calculation of cost per unit of cost driver

Activity	Budgeted cost pool £	Cost driver	Cost driver units pa	Cost per unit of cost driver £
Design department	675,000	Design hours	25,000	27.00
Site engineers	370,000	Miles travelled	185,000	2.00
Purchasing department	105,000	Items purchased	15,000	7.00
Payroll department	75,000	Direct hours	300,000	0.25
Site management	750,000	Direct hours	300,000	2.50
Post-installation inspection	80,000	Items purchased	20,000	4.00

Cost pool	Workings	Total cost HMG/012 £	Total cost CFG/013 £
Design department	£27 × 1,280/620	34,560	16,740
Site engineers	£2 × (320 × 30)/(90 × 10)	19,200	1,800
Purchasing department	£7 × 650/410	4,550	2,870
Payroll department	£0.25 × 10,000/6,000	2,500	1,500
Site management	£2.50 × 10,000/6,000	25,000	15,000
Post-installation inspection	£4 × 650/410	2,600	1,640
Total cost		88,410	39,550

Task 9.2

	Server allocated overheads £	PC allocated overheads £
Set-up costs	10,000	
Rent and power (production area)	24,000	96,000
Rent (stores area)	25,000	25,000
Salaries of stores issue staff	8,000	32,000
Total overheads	67,000	153,000

Workings

Reallocation of Little Ltd's budgeted total fixed annual overheads between server and PC production

Step 1. Calculation of cost per cost driver

	Budgeted total annual overheads	Cost driver	Number of cost drivers	Cost per cost driver
Set-up costs	10,000	Number of set-ups	5	2,000.00
Rent and power (production area)	120,000	Number of wks' production	50	2,400.00
Rent (stores area)	50,000	Floor area of stores (m^2)	800	62.50
Salaries of store issue staff	40,000	No of issues of inventory	10,000	4.00
	220,000			

Step 2. Reallocation of overheads based on costs per cost driver

Server	(i) Number of cost drivers	(ii) Cost per cost driver £	(i) × (ii) Allocated overheads £
Set-up costs	5	2,000.00	10,000
Rent and power (production area)	10	2,400.00	24,000
Rent (stores area)	400	62.50	25,000
Salaries of store issue staff	2,000	4.00	8,000
			67,000

PC	(i) Number of cost drivers	(ii) Cost per cost driver £	(i) × (ii) Allocated overheads £
Set-up costs	0	2,000.00	–
Rent and power (production area)	40	2,400.00	96,000
Rent (stores area)	400	62.50	25,000
Salaries of store issue staff	8,000	4.00	32,000
			153,000

Task 9.3

	Plastic allocated overheads £	Metal allocated overheads £
Power for machinery	50,000	60,000
Rent of factory	100,000	20,000
Canteen costs	32,000	8,000
Total overheads	182,000	88,000

Workings

1 **Calculation of cost per cost driver**

	Budgeted overheads	Cost driver	Number of cost drivers	Cost per cost driver
Power for machinery	110,000	Number of machine hours	5,500	20
Rent of factory	120,000	Floor space	1,200	100
Canteen costs	40,000	Number of employees	250	160

BPP
LEARNING MEDIA

2 **Reallocation of overheads based on costs per cost driver**

Plastic	(i) Number of cost drivers	(ii) Cost per cost driver £	(i) × (ii) Allocated overheads £
Power for machinery	2,500	20	50,000
Rent of factory	1,000	100	100,000
Canteen costs	200	160	32,000
Total			182,000

Metal	(i) Number of cost drivers	(ii) Cost per cost driver £	(i) × (ii) Allocated overheads £
Power for machinery	3,000	20	60,000
Rent of factory	200	100	20,000
Canteen costs	50	160	8,000
Total			88,000

Chapter 10

Task 10.1

The breakeven point in units is | 100,000 | units.

The margin of safety in units is | 15,000 | units.

The margin of safety as a percentage of budgeted sales is | 13 | % .

Workings

1 **Breakeven point** $= \dfrac{£1,100,000}{£28-£17}$

$= 100,000$ units

2 **Margin of safety (units)** $=$ Budgeted sales – Breakeven sales

$= (115,000 - 100,000)$ units

$= 15,000$ units

3 **Margin of safety (% budgeted sales)**

$= \dfrac{115,000 - 100,000}{115,000} \times 100\%$

$= 13\%$

Task 10.2

The breakeven point both in terms of units and sales revenue is:

Units	✓
5,000	✓
10,000	

Sales revenue £	✓
40,000	
80,000	✓

Working:

Contribution per unit = £(16 − 8) = £8

Contribution required to breakeven = fixed costs = £40,000

Breakeven point $= \dfrac{\text{Fixed costs}}{\text{Contribution per unit}}$

$\qquad\qquad = \dfrac{£40,000}{£8}$

$\qquad\qquad = 5,000 \text{ units}$

Sales revenue at breakeven point $\quad = 5,000 \text{ units} \times £16 \text{ per unit}$
$\qquad\qquad\qquad\qquad\qquad\qquad\quad = £80,000$

Task 10.3

The margin of safety, in terms of both units and sales revenue is:

Units	✓
500	✓
2,000	
1,900	
500	

Sales revenue £	✓
12,500	
160,000	
152,000	
40,000	✓

Working:

Margin of safety = Budgeted sales volume − Breakeven sales volume

Breakeven sales volume $\quad = \dfrac{\text{Fixed costs}}{\text{Contribution per unit}}$

$$= \frac{£110,000}{£55}$$

$$= 2,000 \text{ units}$$

Therefore, margin of safety (units) = 2,500 units – 2,000 units

$$= 500 \text{ units}$$

Therefore, margin of safety (sales revenue) = Margin of safety (units) × Selling price per unit

$$= 500 \text{ units} \times £80$$

$$= £40,000$$

Task 10.4

The number of units of the product that the business must sell in order to make a target profit of £300,000 is $\boxed{46,667}$ units.

Working:

Target profit units $= \dfrac{£540,000 + £300,000}{£83 - 65}$

$$= 46,667 \text{ units}$$

Task 10.5

The sales revenue required in order to make a target profit of £250,000 is $\boxed{£ \quad 2,560,000}$.

Working:

Profit volume ratio $= \dfrac{£40 - 28}{£40} \times 100\% = 30\%$

Target profit sales revenue $= \dfrac{£518,000 + £250,000}{0.3} = £2,560,000$

Task 10.6

Product	Units
B	800
A	1,000
C	50

Workings

1   **Contribution per kg**

	A	B	C
Contribution	£12	£16	£16
Kg per unit	2	1	4
Contribution per kg	£6	£16	£4
Ranking	2	1	3

2   **Production plan**

	Units	Kg used	Cumulative kg used
B	800	800	800
A	1,000	2,000	2,800
C (balance)	50	200	3,000
		3,000	

··

Task 10.7

Product	Units
T	8,000
R	20,000
S	12,000

The contribution that will be earned under this production plan is

£ 540,000 .

Workings

1   **Identify the limiting factor**

Materials – at maximum demand

$(4 \times 20,000) + (5 \times 25,000) + (3 \times 8,000) = 229,000$ kg

Labour hours – at maximum demand

$(2 \times 20,000) + (3 \times 25,000) + (3 \times 8,000) = 139,000$ hours

Machine hours – at maximum demand

$(4 \times 20,000) + (3 \times 25,000) + (2 \times 8,000) = 171,000$ hours

Therefore the only limiting factor is labour hours.

2 **Contribution per labour hour**

	R	S	T
Contribution	£11	£14	£19
Labour hours	2	3	3
Contribution per labour hour	£5.50	£4.67	£6.33
Ranking	2	3	1

3 **Production plan**

	Units	Labour hours used	Cumulative labour hours used
T	8,000	24,000	24,000
R	20,000	40,000	64,000
S (balance)	12,000	36,000	100,000
		100,000	

4 **Contribution earned**

	£
R (20,000 × £11)	220,000
S (12,000 × £14)	168,000
T (8,000 × £19)	152,000
	540,000

Task 10.8

(a)

	Product X £	Product Y £
The contribution per unit is	45	57
The contribution per kilogram of materials	7.5	7.13

Workings

Contribution = selling price – variable costs

Contribution for X = £100 – £55 = £45

Contribution for Y = £135 – £78 = £57

Contribution for X per kg of material = £45/$\dfrac{£30}{£5}$ = £7.50

Contribution for Y per kg of material = £57/$\dfrac{£40}{£5}$ = £7.125 = £7.13 to the nearest penny.

(b) The optimal production order for products X, and Y is

product X then product Y .

(c)

	Product X Units	Product Y Units
Production	3,500	3,000

Working: (3,500 × 6kg) + (3,000 × 8kg) = 45,000kg

(d)

	Product X £	Product Y £
Total contribution	157,500	171,000

Task 10.9

(a)

	Product Tig £	Product Tag £
The contribution per unit is	1,200	1,350
The contribution per kilogram of materials is	200	180

Workings

1 **Contribution per unit**

Product Tig = £4,000 – £2,800 = £1,200
Product Tag = £4,950 – £3,600 = £1,350

2 **Contribution per kilogram of material**

Product Tig = £1,200/6kg = £200
Product Tag = £1,350/7.5kg = £180

(b) The optimal production order for products Tig and Tag is [Tig then Tag.]

(based on the contribution per kilogram of material calculated in part (a)).

(c)

	Product Tig Units	Product Tag Units
Production	200	240

Working:

Supply is limited to 3,000 kilograms of material

Product Tig then Tag (based on part (b)).

200 units of Tig × 6kg per unit = 1,200kg (so 1,800kg remaining to produce Tag)

1,800kg/7.5kg per unit = 240 units of Tag

(d)

	Product Tig £	Product Tag £
Total contribution	240,000	324,000

Workings

Product Tig = 200 units × £1,200 = £240,000

Product Tag = 240 units × £1,350 = £324,000

(e)

Should Alpha purchase the additional material?	Give a reason
Yes	The additional cost per kilogram is less than the contribution per kilogram.

Task 10.10

(a)

Product	A	B
Fixed costs (£) (per question)	158,620	105,400
Unit contribution (£) (W)	1.03	0.62
Breakeven sales (units) (Fixed cost/contribution per unit)	154,000	170,000
Forecast sales (units)	250,000	400,000
Margin of safety (units) (Forecast – breakeven sales)	96,000	230,000
Margin of safety (%)	38.40%	57.50%

Workings

1 **Contribution per unit – Product A**

(Sales revenue – variable costs)/number of units = 450,000 – 60,000 – 36,000 – 45,000)/300,000 = £1.03

2 **Contribution per unit – Product B**

(Sales revenue – variable costs)/number of units = 600,000 – 125,000 – 70,000 – 95,000)/500,000 = £0.62

(b) Product B has the better margin of safety.

Product B's sales can fall by 57.5% before it breaks even. Any greater fall than this will result in the company making a loss whereas Product A's sales can only drop by 38.4% before it starts to lose money.

Task 10.11

1,000 units

At this level of forecast sales the company is selling 200 units below what it needs to break even, so there is no margin of safety; it is already making a loss.

1,200 units

At this forecast level of sales the margin of safety is zero as this is the break even level.

Sales cannot fall below this level or else a loss will be made.

1,500 units

At this forecast level of sales the company is making a profit. Sales could drop by 20% before a profit would no longer be made.

The company needs to sell more than 1,200 units.

Task 10.12

The net present value of the investment is | £ | (5,682) |.

Workings

Net present value

Year	Cash flow £	Discount factor @ 7%	Present value £
0	(84,000)	1.000	(84,000)
1	26,000	0.935	24,310
2	30,000	0.873	26,190
3	21,000	0.816	17,136
4	14,000	0.763	10,682
Net present value			(5,682)

Task 10.13

The net present value of the potential investment is:

£	41,591

Workings

Net present value

Year	Cash flow £	Discount factor @ 12%	Present value £
0	(355,000)	1.000	(355,000)
1 (47 + 60)	107,000	0.893	95,551
2 (55 + 60)	115,000	0.797	91,655
3 (68 + 60)	128,000	0.712	91,136
4 (53 + 60)	113,000	0.635	71,755
5 (22 + 60)	82,000	0.567	46,494
Net present value			41,591

Note. Depreciation is not a cash flow and having been charged in arriving at the profit figure must be added back to find the cash inflow in each year.

··

Task 10.14

(a)

	Year					
	0	1	2	3	4	5
Cash flow (£)	(400,000)	(50,000)	(52,500)	(55,125)	(55,125)	(20,125)
Discounted factor	1	0.952	0.907	0.864	0.823	0.784
Present value (£)	(400,000)	(47,600)	(47,618)*	(47,628)	(45,368)*	(15,778)
Net present cost (£)	(603,992)					

Notes

1   The question states that you should 'round to the nearest whole pound'.

     The figures are clearly signposted in the question.

2   Year 5 cash flow figure includes the cash inflow for the residual value, so is calculated as £55,125 – £35,000 = £20,125.

(b)

| | **Year** | | | | | |
	0	**1**	**2**	**3**	**4**	**5**
Cash flow (£)	(140,000)	(140,000)	(140,000)	(140,000)	(140,000)	0
Discounted factor	1	0.952	0.907	0.864	0.823	0.784
Present value (£)	(140,000)	(133,280)	(126,980)	(120,960)	(115,220)	0
Net present cost (£)	(636,440)					

Workings

Ensure you enter the annual lease payments in the correct years. The lease fee is paid in advance (so the Year 1 fee is paid in Year 0). The lease is for five years, so the final year fee will be paid in advance in Year 4.

(c)   Based on the calculations it is best to ⎸ purchase ⎸ as this saves

£ | 32,448 | .

Working: £636,440 – £603,992 = £32,448

AAT AQ2016 SAMPLE ASSESSMENT 1
MANAGEMENT ACCOUNTING:
DECISION AND CONTROL

Time allowed: 2 hours and 30 minutes

The AAT may call the assessments on their website, under study support resources, either a 'practice assessment' or 'sample assessment'.

Management Accounting: Decision and Control
AAT sample assessment 1

Task 1 (12 marks)

A manufacturer of a single product has supplied the budget information below for the next quarter end.

Materials per unit   2.55 kg at £3.20 per kg
Rent per quarter   £7,450
Leased machines   £7,522 for every 5,000 units produced
Maintenance   £2,150 per quarter plus £2.07 per unit

(a) **Calculate the budgeted quarterly costs of production for 15,900 units to the nearest pound (£), and classify each cost using the dropdown boxes.** (8 marks)

	Quarterly production		
Cost	3,800 units £	15,900 units £	Cost Classification
Direct materials	31,008		▼
Rent	7,450		▼
Leased machines	7,522		▼
Maintenance	10,016		▼

Drop-down list:

Fixed
Semi-variable
Stepped
Variable

You have been supplied with the following information about a factory's overheads:

Units produced	Total overheads £
19,000	295,000
23,900	324,400

The fixed portion of the overheads increases by £12,000 when more than 30,000 units are produced.

Variable costs decrease by £1 per unit for units produced in excess of 25,000 units.

(b) Calculate the total fixed and variable overheads for the following production levels.

Enter your answers to the nearest pound (£).   **(4 marks)**

Units	Fixed £	Variable £
21,000		
36,000		

....

Task 2   (15 marks)

The production information below relates to Apricot Ltd, a business that packages apricots:

	Budget	Actual
Production (cartons)	5,000	6,000
Apricots (kg)	50,000	70,000
Apricots (£)	25,000	36,000
Direct labour (hours)	1,000	800
Direct labour (£)	10,000	8,000

(a) (i) Calculate the variances in the table below. Enter your answers to the nearest whole pound (£). Enter a zero if there is no variance. Do not use minus signs or brackets.
(7 marks)

(ii) Use the dropdown boxes to indicate whether each variance you calculate in (i) is adverse, favourable or no variance.
(4 marks)

	£	Adverse/Favourable/No variance
Apricots price variance	5,000	▼
Apricots usage variance		▼
Direct labour rate variance	0	▼
Direct labour efficiency variance		▼

Drop-down list:

Adverse
Favourable
No variance

A company manufactures Product DD.

Each unit of product DD is budgeted to require 2 hours of labour at a cost of £18 per hour. The company manufactured 950 units and the labour efficiency variance was £180 adverse.

(b) **Calculate the actual number of hours used to produce 950 units to the nearest whole number.** **(2 marks)**

The actual number of hours used was ☐.

The product is budgeted to use 1.25 kg of material per unit at a cost of £7.80 per kg.

During last month the company used 1.140 kg to manufacture 950 units and the material price variance was £912 adverse.

(c) **Calculate the actual price per kg of material to two decimal places.** **(2 marks)**

The actual price per kg of material was £ ☐

Task 3   (15 marks)

The following budgeted figures refer to a factory producing a single product.

Overheads are absorbed on a budgeted production basis.

Inventory is valued on a FIFO basis.

	Month 1	Month 2	Month 3
Operating inventory (units)	0		
Selling price (£)	110	100	90
Production (units)	10,000	10,000	10,000
Sales (units)	8,000	9,000	11,000
Direct materials (£ per unit)	15	15	15
Direct labour (£ per unit)	10	10	10
Other variable production costs (£)	230,000	230,000	250,000
Fixed production costs (£)	450,000	450,000	450,000

Complete the budgeted operating profit statement below for month 3 using absorption costing and marginal costing.

Apply the appropriate standard cost for the valuation of production and inventory. Use positive numbers only for the sales to fixed overheads rows. Do not use minus signs or brackets.

For the final row, record any loss figure with a minus sign.

If any answer is zero or a figure is not required, enter '0' into the relevant cell.   **(15 marks)**

	Absorption costing Month 3 £	Marginal costing Month 3 £
Sales – month 3		
Opening inventory		
Production costs		
Closing inventory		
Cost of sales		
Fixed overheads		
Profit/(Loss)		

Task 4 (12 marks)

(a) **A retail shop analyses its sales volumes using Time Series Analysis. Enter the appropriate three-month moving averages for sales units into the table below.** (3 marks)

Month	Sales Units	Three-month moving average Units
December	5,760	
January	5,820	
February	5,760	
March	6,600	
April	6,120	
May	6,150	
June	6,330	

(b) **Complete the following sentences: using the dropdown boxes to indicate your answers.** (2 marks)

Seasonal variation equals actual sales for a month, less [▼] sales for the same month.

Drop-down list:

cost
indexed
trend

The observation that retail sales are higher during November and December

is an example of [▼] .

Drop-down list:

random variation
seasonal variation
trend

The information below relates to production costs and the Retail Price Index (RPI).

(c) **Complete the table below by restating the following costs at January prices. Enter the costs to the nearest pound (£).**

(3 marks)

Month	Actual costs £	RPI	Costs at January prices £
January	129,000	170	
March	132,000	172	
June	135,000	174	

The retail shop's delivery costs vary in a linear manner and can be expressed using the regression equation y = a + bx, where x = the number of units delivered.

The total delivery costs for 200 units and 2,000 units are £5,000 and £14,000 respectively.

(d) **Calculate the values of a and b.**　　　　　　　　**(4 marks)**

Value of a: ⬚

Value of b: ⬚

Task 5   (18 marks)

Ezo Ltd (a manufacturer of hi-tech electrical parts) has supplied its operating statement for last month, which reconciles the standard cost of actual production with the actual cost of production.

	£	Adverse /Favourable
Standard cost of actual production	600,000	
Variances		
Materials price	5,000	Adv
Materials usage	7,000	Fav
Labour rate	10,000	Adv
Labour efficiency	10,000	Fav
Fixed overhead expenditure	7,000	Fav
Fixed overhead volume	11,000	Fav
Actual cost of production	600,000	

Recent events

Storage facilities:

Alternative storage facilities were rented at the beginning of last month leading to lower monthly payments.

Machinery:

At the beginning of last month, an investment was made in more modern and efficient machinery which has a slightly smaller monthly depreciation charge.

Staff upgrade:

Ezo Ltd recruited skilled machine operators to operate the machinery at the start of last month. Exo Ltd made the existing unskilled workers redundant at the same time. The unskilled workers had been notified of their redundancy three months ago

(a) For EACH of the following variances, explain how they could have been affected by the information above:

- Materials variances
- Labour variances
- Fixed overhead variances   (12 marks)

(b) **Explain why the following standards may need to be amended in Ezo Ltd's standard cost card in order to make variance analysis more effective in the future.**

Material standards (2 marks)

Labour standards (2 marks)

Fixed overhead standards (2 marks)

Task 6 (15 marks)

(a) **Complete the statement below:** (1 mark)

Reducing the cost of a product without reducing its value to the customer is

an example of removing a [　　　　▼] activity.

Drop-down list:
benchmark
non-value-added
value-added

(b) **Complete the following statement:** (1 mark)

The "innovation and learning perspective" is associated with the concept of

[　　　▼].

Drop-down list:

efficiency
the balanced scorecard
value-added

A small business has supplied the following information:

	£
Turnover	1,500,000
Cost of materials used	700,000
Cost of bought in services	300,000
Number of employees	10

(c) **Use the information provided to complete the statements below:** (2 marks)

The total value added is £ [　　　　　].

Value added per employee is a measure of [　　　　▼].

Drop-down list:
capacity
net profit
productivity

A business with receivables of £120,000 and receivables collection period of 30 days, operates on a gross profit margin of 25% and a net profit margin of 15%. Fixed production overheads constitute 40% of the cost of sales.

(d) **Complete the profit and loss account below using the performance indicators given above.**

Enter ALL figures as positive numbers – do not enter negative figures. Assume 365 days in one year. **(9 marks)**

	£
Sales	
Variable production costs	
Fixed production costs	
Cost of sales	
Gross profit	
Non-production costs	
Net profit	

(e) **Based on your calculations in (d), if payables are £117,000, what is the payables period to the nearest day?** **(2 marks)**

days

. . . .

Task 7 **(18 marks)**

A company manufactures two products, the Jackal and the Hyena.

The information below relates to the next reporting period:

Per unit	Jackal £	Hyena £
Direct materials at £5 per kg	10	15
Direct labour at £6 per hour	6	12
Variable overheads	2	4
Selling price	25	40
	Units	**Units**
Sales demand	5,000	11,000

290

As a result of recent transport strikes, materials are limited to 55,000 kg and labour hours are limited to 20,000.

(a) **(i)** **Complete the table below for the next reporting period by calculating the missing figures for Jackal and Hyena.**

(6 marks)

	Jackal	Hyena
Contribution per unit (£)		
Contribution per limiting factor (£) (to TWO decimal places)		
Optimal production (units)		

(ii) **Explain why you have chosen the production levels you gave in answer (i) and the consequences of choosing a different level of production. You may use calculations to support your answer.** **(7 marks)**

A company is considering purchasing new equipment and has drawn up a comparison of the current situation and the proposed situation with the new equipment.

	Current situation	Proposed situation with new equipment
Direct materials per unit	3 kg at £5	15% decrease in usage
Direct labour per unit	6 hours at £10	20% decrease in hours
Sales	5,000 units at £150	No change
Fixed costs	£277,500	Increase of £79,500

(b) (i) Calculate the profit figures for the current and proposed situation. **(4 marks)**

	Current situation £	Proposed situation with new equipment £
Profit		

(ii) Complete the sentence below to state whether or not the new equipment should be acquired. Use the dropdown box to select your answer. **(1 mark)**

It [▼] be better to acquire the new equipment.

Drop-down list:

would
would not

Task 8   (15 marks)

Herb Ltd manufactures two products, Rose and Thyme.

The budgeted cost for the two overhead activities is as follows:

- Materials handling £400,000
- Production set-ups £600,000

Further information has been provided below.

	Rose	Thyme
Direct materials – £ per unit	2.10	3.33
Direct labour – £ per unit	30	20
Direct labour – hours per unit	3	2
Number of material requisitions	400	1,200
Number of production set-ups	150	450
Budgeted production – units	50,000	25,000

(a) **Complete the table below using activity based costing (ABC) principles.** **(6 marks)**

	Rose £	Thyme £	Total overheads £
Cost driver – per material requisition			
Cost driver – per production set-up			
Total materials handling			400,000
Total production set-ups			600,000

(b) **Using the information supplied in (a), calculate the fixed overheads assuming they are absorbed on a budgeted labour hours basis.** **(2 marks)**

	Rose £	Thyme £
Fixed overheads		

The total cost per unit under the two different methods to two decimal places is shown in the table below.

	Rose £	Thyme £
Total unit cost – ABC	37.10	53.33
Total unit cost – labour hours	47.10	33.33

(c) **Discuss the advantages and disadvantages of moving to an ABC system for the company.** **(7 marks)**

AAT AQ2016 SAMPLE ASSESSMENT 1 MANAGEMENT ACCOUNTING: DECISION AND CONTROL

ANSWERS

Management Accounting: Decision and Control
AAT sample assessment 1

Task 1   (12 marks)

(a) Calculate the budgeted quarterly costs of production for 15,900 units to the nearest pound (£) and classify each cost using the dropdown boxes   (8 marks)

Cost	Quarterly production 3,800 units £	15,900 units £	Cost Classification
Direct materials	31,008	129,744	Variable
Rent	7,450	7,450	Fixed
Leased machines	7,522	30,088	Stepped
Maintenance	10,016	35,063	Semi-variable

(b) Calculate the total fixed and variable overheads for the following production levels. Enter your answers to the nearest pound (£).   (4 marks)

Units	Fixed £	Variable £
21,000	181,000	126,000
36,000	193,000	205,000

Task 2 **(15 marks)**

(a)   (i)   Calculate the variances in the table below. Enter your answers to the nearest whole pound (£). Enter a zero if there is no variance. Do not use minus signs or brackets. **(7 marks)**

(ii) Use the dropdown boxes to indicate whether each variance you calculate in (i) is adverse, favourable or no variance. **(4 marks)**

	£	Adverse/ Favourable/ No variance
Apricots price variance	1,000	Adverse
Apricots usage variance	5,000	Adverse
Direct labour rate variance	0	No variance
Direct labour efficiency variance	4,000	Favourable

(b)   Calculate the actual number of hours used to produce 950 units to the nearest whole number. **(2 marks)**

The actual number of hours used was ┌─────────┐ 1,910 └─────────┘ .

(c)   Calculate the actual price per kg of the material to two decimal places. **(2 marks)**

The actual price per kg of material was £ │ 8.60

Task 3 (15 marks)

(a) **Complete the budgeted operating profit statement below for month 3, using absorption costing and marginal costing.**

Apply the appropriate standard cost for the valuation of production and inventory. Use positive numbers only for the sales to fixed overheads rows. Do not use minus signs or brackets.

For the final row, record any loss figure with minus sign. If any answer is zero or a figure is not required, enter '0' into the relevant cell. (15 marks)

	Absorption costing Month 3 £	Marginal costing Month 3 £
Sales – month 3	990,000	990,000
Opening inventory	279,000	144,000
Production costs	950,000	500,000
Closing inventory	190,000	100,000
Cost of sales	1,039,000	544,000
Fixed overheads	0	450,000
Profit/Loss	–49,000	–4,000

Task 4 (12 marks)

(a) A retail shop analyses its sales volumes using Time Series Analysis. Enter the appropriate three month moving averages for sales units into the table below. (3 marks)

Month	Sales Units	Three month moving average Units
December	5,760	
January	5,820	5,780
February	5,760	
March	6,600	6,160
April	6,120	
May	6,150	6,200
June	6,330	

(b) Complete the following sentences using the dropdown boxes to indicate your answer. (2 marks)

Seasonal variation equals sales for month, less ⌊ trend ⌋ sales for the same month.

The observation that retail sales are higher during November and December is an example of ⌊ seasonal variation ⌋.

(c) Complete the table below by restating the following costs at January prices. Enter the costs to the nearest pound (£). (3 marks)

Month	Actual cost £	RPI	Cost at January prices £
January	129,000	170	129,000
March	132,000	172	130,264
June	135,000	174	131,897

(d) **Calculate the value of a and b.** **(4 marks)**

Value of a: 4,000

Value of b: 5

· ·

Task 5 (18 marks)

> The notes below cover a range of possible points that you may include in your written response. These examples are not intended to be exhaustive and other valid comments may be relevant.

(a) **For EACH of the following variances, explain how they could have been affected by the information above:**

- **Materials variances**
- **Labour variances**
- **Fixed overhead variances.** **(12 marks)**

Material variances

The general price of materials may have risen since the budget was set. Also, a higher quality of material may have been purchased to be used in the new machinery. Both factors would lead to the adverse price variance of £5k.

The new machinery is likely to manufacture the finished product more effectively with less waste. Similarly, the new highly skilled labour will be able to handle the raw materials more effectively with less waste. Both will lead to a favourable usage variance (here £7k).

Labour variances

The new higher skilled workers will be paid a higher hourly rate. The redundancy costs for the less skilled workers may have been included in this month's wages costs. Both would explain the £10k adverse rate variance.

Higher skilled workers will be more efficient overall, capable of producing more components per hour. They may also be highly motivated as they had just been recruited to new roles. These would lead to a favourable efficiency variance here of £10k.

Fixed overhead variances

The £7k favourable expenditure variance can be explained by the reduction in rent and the lower depreciation charge on the new machinery. Both would have reduced overall fixed overhead expenditure in comparison to the original budget.

The efficiency of the new machine could improve productive capacity. Coupled with the higher skilled labour, which is likely to be able to produce more in their working week, more units would have been produced than expected. Therefore the volume variance is £11k favourable.

(b) **Explain why the following standards may need to be amended in Ezo Ltd's standard cost card in order to make variance analysis more effective in the future.**

Material standards **(2 marks)**

The standard material price may need to be amended to reflect different price of input material. If the material is of higher quality, the standard material usage may need to be reduced to reflect standard input material quantity is less for the new machine.

Labour standards **(2 marks)**

Higher skilled labour is likely to take less time to make each unit. Therefore the standard labour hours per unit could fall. They are also likely to have a higher wage rate and therefore a higher standard cost per hour.

Fixed Overhead standards **(2 marks)**

The saving in rent on the storage facilities will reduce the standard fixed cost expenditure in total. Additionally, any long-term increase in expected production levels will reduce the standard fixed overhead per unit.

Task 6 **(15 marks)**

(a) **Complete the statement below.** **(1 mark)**

Reducing the cost of a product without reducing its value to the costumer is and example of removing a | non-value-added | activity.

(b) **Complete the following statement.** **(1 mark)**

The "innovation and learning perspective" is associated with the concept of | the balanced scorecard | .

(c) **Use the information provided to complete the statement below.** **(2 marks)**

The total value added is | £ | 500,000 | .

Value added per employee is a measure of | productivity | .

(d) **Complete the profit and loss account below using the performance indicators given above.**

Enter ALL figures as positive numbers – do not enter negative figures. Assume 365 days is one year. **(9 marks)**

	£
Sales	1,460,000
Variable production costs	657,000
Fixed production costs	438,000
Cost of sales	1,095,000
Gross profit	365,000
Non-production costs	146,000
Operating profit	219,000

(e) **Based on your calculation in (d), if payables are £117,000, what is the payables period to the nearest day?** **(2 marks)**

| 39 | days. |

....

Task 7 (18 marks)

(a) **(i)** **Complete the table below for the next reporting period by calculating the missing figures for Jackal and Hyena.**

(6 marks)

	Jackal	Hyena
Contribution per unit (£)	7	9
Contribution per limiting factor (£) (to TWO decimal places)	7.00	4.50
Optimal production (units)	5,000	7,500

The notes below cover a range of possible points that you may include in your written response.

These examples are not intended to be exhaustive and other valid comments may be relevant.

(ii) **Explain why you have chosen the production levels you gave in answer (i) and the consequences of choosing a different level of production. You may use calculations to support your answer.** **(7 marks)**

If the company were to produce the total sales demand they would require 43,000kg of material (which they have) and 27,000 labour hours (which they don't have).

This means they need to make the best possible use of the scarce resource (1 mark), in this case, labour hours.

To do this we calculate the contribution per limiting factor and produce in order of the best return in terms of the limiting factor. If we do not do this and produce any other quantity we will have less contribution and therefore less profit.

Optimum production gives contribution of £102,500 (£35,000 + £67,500) whereas producing Hyena first would give a contribution of £90,000.

(b) **(i)** **Calculate the profit figures for the current and proposed situation.** **(4 marks)**

	Current situation £	Proposed situation with new equipment £
Profit	97,500	89,250

(ii) **Complete the sentence below to state whether or not the new equipment should be acquired.**

Used the dropdown box to select your answer. **(1 mark)**

It | would not | be better to acquire the new equipment.

Task 8 (15 marks)

(a) **Complete the table below using Activity Based Costing (ABC) principles.** (6 marks)

£	£	Rose £	Thyme £	Total overheads £
Cost driver – per material requisition	250			
Cost driver – per production set-up	1,000			
Total materials handling		100,000	300,000	400,000
Total production set-ups		150,000	450,000	600,000

(b) **Using the information in (a), calculate the fixed overheads assuming they are absorbed on a budgeted labour hours basis.** (2 marks)

	Rose £	Thyme £
Fixed overhead	750,000	250,000

The notes below cover a range of possible points that you may include in your written response.

These examples are not intended to be exhaustive and other valid comments may be relevant.

(c) **Discuss the advantages and disadvantages of moving to an ABC system for the company.** (7 marks)

Using ABC leads to more accurate product costs using a fairer allocation of the overheads charged. This leads to better decision making in terms of pricing, withdrawal of products, and production scheduling. It's also believed that ABC leads to better management understanding of the cause and allocation of overheads.

By identifying the cost pools, management are able to look at ways to achieve savings in overheads in a more focused way. By using cost drivers, management can assess whether product profitability can be increased by reducing the number of times a driver is used.

The time taken to identify activities and install the system could be a disadvantage for the company. The cost of implementation and the cost of running the system may also be a disadvantage. Another disadvantage for the company could be any resistance to change that they encounter.

AAT AQ2016 SAMPLE ASSESSMENT 2 MANAGEMENT ACCOUNTING: DECISION AND CONTROL

Time allowed: 2 hours and 30 minutes

You are advised to attempt sample assessment 2 online from the AAT website. This will ensure you are prepared for how the assessment will be presented on the AAT's system when you attempt the real assessment. Please access the assessment using the address below:

https://www.aat.org.uk/training/study-support/search

The AAT may call the assessments on their website, under study support resources, either a 'practice assessment' or 'sample assessment'.

BPP PRACTICE ASSESSMENT 1
MANAGEMENT ACCOUNTING: DECISION AND CONTROL

Time allowed: 2 hours and 30 minutes

PRACTICE ASSESSMENT 1

Management Accounting: Decision & Control
BPP practice assessment 1

Task 1 (12 marks)

RD Ltd manufactures rubberised asphalt and operates a standard costing system.

The standard cost card for the coming month is being prepared and you have been given the following information.

- 50 tonnes of CR materials will be transferred from the CR Division of the company at a cost of £474 per tonne.

- 200 tonnes of asphalt material will be purchased at a cost of £150 per tonne.

- Labour required to produce 250 tonnes of output is 800 hours.

- Labour cost is £10 per hour.

- Fixed running costs of the machines are £150,000 per month.

- Budgeted production is 250 tonnes per month.

- Fixed production overheads are absorbed on the basis of tonnes.

(a) **Complete the standard cost card for the production of 250 tonnes of rubberised asphalt.** **(10 marks)**

	Quantity	Unit price £	Total cost £
CR materials (tonnes)			
Asphalt (tonnes)			
Direct labour (hours)			
Fixed production overheads (tonnes)			
Standard cost			

(b)   Classify the labour cost using the picklist below.

(2 marks)

[_____ ▼]

Picklist:

Fixed
Semi-variable
Stepped
Variable

Task 2   **(15 marks)**

The budgeted activity and actual results for a business for the month of May 20X8 are as follows:

		Budget		**Actual**
Production (tonnes)		200		210
Direct labour	600 hours	£4,800	600 hours	£5,100

(a)   (i)   Complete the following sentences: (2 marks)

The standard labour rate per hour is £ [_____] .

The standard labour hours for actual production is [_____] hours.

(ii)   Calculate the two variances below to the nearest whole pound (£) and indicate whether the variance is adverse, favourable or no variance.   (6 marks)

	Variance £	**Adverse/Favourable**
Direct labour rate variance		
Direct labour efficiency variance		

Another business has a single product into which fixed overheads are absorbed on the basis of labour hours. The standard cost card shows that fixed overheads are to be absorbed on the basis of 8 labour hours per unit at a rate of £10.00 per hour. The budgeted level of production is 100,000 units.

The actual results for the period were that fixed overheads were £7,800,000 and that the actual hours worked were 820,000 and the actual units produced were 98,000.

(b)   Calculate the following variances: **(5 marks)**

	Variance £	Adverse/Favourable
Fixed overhead expenditure variance		
Fixed overhead volume variance		

A company manufactures a product called the Petal. The Petal requires 4 hours of labour at £10 per hour = £40 per unit. During the period, 1,000 units of Petal were made and the variable overhead efficiency variance was £2,000 favourable.

(c)   How long did the 1,000 units of Petal actually take to produce?   **(2 marks)**

| | hours

···

Task 3   **(15 marks)**

ABC Ltd manufactures one product, the ZZ. The company operates a standard costing system and analysis of variances is made every month. The standard cost card for the ZZ is as follows:

	£
Direct materials 0.5 kg at £4.00 per kg	2.00
Direct wages 2 hours at £8.00 per hour	16.00
Variable overheads 2 hours at £0.30 per hour	0.60
	18.60

The budgeted production was for 5,100 units in the month of June. The actual costs during the month of June for the production of 4,850 units were as follows:

	£
Direct materials 2,300 kg	9,800
Direct labour 8,500 hours paid	£67,800
Actual operating hours amounted to 8,000 hours	
Variable overheads	2,600

The following variances have been calculated:

	£
Materials price	600 (A)
Materials usage	500 (F)
Labour rate	200 (F)
Labour efficiency	13,600 (F)
Idle time variance	4,000 (A)
Variable overhead expenditure	200 (A)
Variable overhead efficiency	510 (F)

Calculate the standard cost of 4,850 units of production and insert the variances in the correct place in the following operating statement. Total the variances and reconcile the standard cost of actual production to the actual cost of actual production. (15 marks)

			Total £
Standard cost of actual production			
Variances	**Favourable £**	**Adverse £**	
Materials price			
Materials usage			
Labour rate			
Labour efficiency			
Labour idle time			
Variable overhead expenditure			
Variable overhead efficiency			
Total variances			
Actual cost of actual production			

Task 4 (12 marks)

A company imports tea from India and the historical cost per kilogram is shown below.

	June X7 £	July X7 £	Aug X7 £	Sept X7 £	Oct X7 £	Nov X7 £
Cost per kg of tea	4.95	4.97	4.99	5.05	5.08	5.10

The price per kilogram at January 20X7 was £4.80.

(a) **Convert the costs per kilogram for June and November to index numbers using January 20X7 as the base year (to 2 dp).**
(4 marks)

	£
June cost	
November cost	

It is expected that the index number for tea for January 20X8 will be 108.25.

(b) **What is the expected cost per kilogram for January 20X8 (to 2 dp)?** **(2 marks)**

	✓
£5.52	
£5.36	
£5.20	
£5.40	

(c) **The percentage increase in the price of tea from January 20X7 to January 20X8 is:** **(2 marks)**

	✓
8.33%	
7.69%	
5.80%	
5.58%	

Another company is looking at its packaging costs which seem to vary in a linear manner. If 120,000 units are produced in a month, the costs are £75,000. If 160,000 units are produced in a month then the costs are £95,000. The costs can be predicted using the linear regression equation y = a + bx, where:

x = number of units manufactured

y = the total packaging cost at that level

(d)   Calculate the values of a and b.   **(4 marks)**

Value of a:

£	

Value of b:

£	

Task 5   **(18 marks)**

You are employed as part of the management accounting team in a large industrial company. The production director, who has only recently been appointed, is unfamiliar with fixed overhead variances and standard setting for labour costs. Because of this, the group management accountant has asked you to prepare a report to the production director.

Your report should do the following:

(a)   Outline the similarities and differences between fixed overhead variances and other cost variances such as the material and labour variances.   **(6 marks)**

(b)   Explain what is meant by the fixed overhead total, expenditure and volume variances.   **(6 marks)**

(c)   Explain what factors should be taken into account when setting the standard cost of labour for a product.   **(6 marks)**

Similarities between fixed overhead variances and other variances

The meaning of fixed overhead variances

Setting the standard cost of labour for a product

Task 6 (15 marks)

Given below is a summary of the performance of a business for the last two years:

	20X6 £000	20X7 £000
Sales	1,420	1,560
Cost of sales	850	950
Expenses	370	407
Interest	–	7
Share capital and reserves	1,500	1,600
Long term loan	–	100
Non-current assets	1,100	1,300
Receivables	155	198
Inventory	105	140
Payables	140	162
Bank balance	280	224

For each of the two years complete the table to calculate the performance measures. Give your answers to TWO decimal places.

	20X6	20X7
Gross profit margin		
Operating profit margin		
Return on capital employed		
Asset turnover		
Non-current asset turnover		
Current ratio		
Quick ratio		
Receivables' collection period		
Inventory holding in days		
Payables' payment period		

Task 7 (18 marks)

A company makes three products with the following standard cost information, and predicted maximum sales demand:

- The material available in the coming period is 8,000 kg
- The labour hours available in the coming period are 2,000 hours

	Product		
	A	B	C
Direct materials @ £3 per kg	£9	£6	£12
Direct labour @ £12 per hour	£6	£12	£18
Selling price	£20	£30	£40
Maximum sales demand	1,000 units	800 units	600 units

(a) **Complete the table to determine the production plan which will maximise contribution.** **(11 marks)**

Product	Units

(b) **Suggest possible measures to overcome shortages in materials or labour resources in the period.** **(7 marks)**

Task 8 (15 marks)

(a) **Explain the concept of lifecycle costing?** **(6 marks)**

HM Ltd is considering purchasing a new machine to reduce the labour time taken to produce one of its products. The machine would cost £300,000. The labour time would be reduced from five hours to two hours without compromising quality and the failure rates will remain at zero.

The discount factors you will need are shown below:

Year	Discount factor 5%
0	1.000
1	0.952
2	0.907
3	0.864
4	0.823
5	0.784

(b) **Calculate the discounted lifecycle cost of the machine based upon the following:** **(9 marks)**

    (i) **Purchase price of £300,000**
    (ii) **Annual running costs of £30,000 for the next 5 years**
    (iii) **A residual value of £50,000 at the end of the 5 years**

	Year					
	0 £000	**1** £000	**2** £000	**3** £000	**4** £000	**5** £000
Purchase price						
Running cost						
Residual value						
Net cost						
Discount factor						
Present cost						

The discounted lifecycle cost of the machine is £ _____ .

BPP PRACTICE ASSESSMENT 1
MANAGEMENT ACCOUNTING:
DECISION AND CONTROL

ANSWERS

Management Accounting: Decision & Control
BPP practice assessment 1

Task 1 (12 marks)

(a) Standard cost card for production of 250 tonnes of rubberised asphalt:

	Quantity	Unit price £	Total cost £
CR material (tonnes)	50	474	23,700
Asphalt (tonnes)	200	150	30,000
Direct labour (hours)	800	10	8,000
Fixed production overheads (tonnes)	250	600	150,000
Standard cost			211,700

(b) Labour cost is a **variable cost**.

··

Task 2 (15 marks)

(a) The standard labour rate per hour is **£** 8

The standard labour hours for actual production is 630 hours.

The direct labour rate variance is **£** 300 Adverse.

The direct labour efficiency variance is **£** 240 Favourable.

Workings

Standard labour rate per hour	=	Budgeted labour cost/Budgeted labour hours
	=	£4,800/600
	=	£8 per hour
Standard labour hours for actual production	=	Standard labour hour per tonne × Actual production
	=	600 hours/200 tonnes × 210 tonnes
	=	630 hours

Direct labour rate variance

	£
600 should have cost (× £8)	4,800
But did cost	5,100
Labour rate variance	300 (A)

Direct labour efficiency variance

210 tonnes should have taken (× 3)	630 hours
But did take	600 hours
Efficiency variance in hours	30 (F)
× Standard rate per hour	× £8
Labour efficiency variance	240 (F)

(b)

	Variance £	Adverse/Favourable
Fixed overhead expenditure variance	200,000	Favourable
Fixed overhead volume variance	160,000	Adverse

Workings

1 **Fixed overhead expenditure variance**

	£
Budgeted fixed overhead 100,000 units × 8 hours × £10.00	8,000,000
Actual fixed overhead	7,800,000
Expenditure variance	200,000 (F)

2   **Fixed overhead volume variance**

Budgeted production	100,000 units
Actual production	98,000 units
	2,000 (A)
@ OAR per unit	× £80.00
Volume variance	£160,000 (A)

(c) ⏐ 3,800 ⏐ hours

Working

Variance in hours = £2,000 / £10 = 200 hours. Actual hours taken = 4,000 hours − 200 hours = 3,800 hours

Variable overhead efficiency variance

	£
Actual units should take (1,000 × 4 hours)	4,000 hrs
Actual units did take (balancing figure)	3,800 hrs
	200 (F)
× Standard cost per hour	£10
Variable overhead efficiency variance	£2,000 (F)

Task 3 (15 marks)

	Favourable £	Adverse £	Total £
Standard cost of actual production (4,850 units × £18.60)			90,210
Variances	**Favourable £**	**Adverse £**	
Materials price		600	
Materials usage	500		
Labour rate	200		
Labour efficiency	13,600		
Labour idle time		4,000	
Variable overhead expenditure		200	
Variable overhead efficiency	510		
Total variances	14,810	4,800	10,010 (F)
Actual cost of actual production (9,800 + 67,800 +2,600)			80,200

Task 4 (12 marks)

(a)

	£
June cost	103.13
November cost	106.25

June $= \dfrac{£4.95}{£4.80} \times 100 = 103.13$

November $= \dfrac{£5.10}{£4.80} \times 100 = 106.25$

(b)

	✓
£5.52	
£5.36	
£5.20	✓
£5.40	

January X8 cost = $\dfrac{£4.80 \times 108.25}{100}$ = £5.20

(c)

	✓
8.33%	✓
7.69%	
5.80%	
5.58%	

Percentage increase = $\dfrac{£5.20 - £4.80}{£4.80} \times 100$

= 8.33%

(d) a = | £ | 15,000 |

b = | £ | 0.50 |

Using the high low method we can calculate the variable cost per unit (b).

(£95,000 – £75,000) /(160,000 – 120,000) = £0.50

Then we can calculate the fixed costs (a).

£95,000 – (160,000 × £0.50) = £15,000

Task 5 (18 marks)

REPORT

To: Production Director
From: Assistant Management Accountant
Date: xx/xx/xx
Subject: Fixed overhead variances and standard setting

This memorandum provides information on fixed overhead variances. In particular it covers the similarities between fixed overhead variances and other cost variances, the meaning of the various fixed overhead variances and the ways in which such variances can be of assistance in the planning and the controlling of the division.

Similarities between fixed overhead variances and other variances

The fixed overhead expenditure variance is the difference between the budgeted fixed overhead expenditure and actual fixed overhead expenditure.

It is therefore similar to the material price and labour rate variances in that it shows the effect on costs and hence profit of paying more or less than anticipated for resources used.

Material usage and labour efficiency variances show the effect on costs and hence profit of having used more or less resource than should have been used for the actual volume of production. Fixed overheads should remain constant within the relevant range of production, however; they should not change simply because budgeted and actual production volumes differ. Fixed overhead variances similar to material usage and labour efficiency variances (reflecting the difference between the actual fixed overhead expenditure and the fixed overhead expenditure which should have been incurred at the actual volume of production) cannot therefore occur.

The meaning of fixed overhead variances

Whereas labour and material total variances show the effect on costs and hence profit of the difference between what the actual production volume should have cost and what it did cost (in terms of labour or material), if an organisation uses standard absorption costing (as we do), the fixed overhead total variance is the difference between actual fixed overhead expenditure and the fixed overhead absorbed (the under- or over-absorbed overhead).

The total under- or over-absorption is made up of the fixed overhead expenditure variance and the fixed overhead volume variance. The expenditure variance measures the difference between the budgeted and actual fixed production overhead incurred. The volume variance shows that part of the under- or over-absorbed overhead which is due to any difference between budgeted production volume and actual production volume.

Setting the standard cost of labour for a product

The standard cost of the direct labour for a product will be made up of:

- The amount of time being spent on each unit of the product
- The hourly wage rate for the employees working on the product

Factors that should be taken into account when setting the standard for the amount of labour time include:

- The level of skill or training of the labour used on the product
- Any anticipated changes in the grade of labour used on the product
- Any anticipated changes in work methods or productivity levels
- The effect on productivity of any bonus scheme to be introduced

The hourly rate for the direct labour used on the product can be found from the payroll records. However, consideration should be given to:

- Anticipated pay rises
- Any anticipated changes in the grade of labour to be used
- The effect of any bonus scheme on the labour rate
- Whether any overtime is anticipated and should be built into the hourly rate

··

Task 6 (15 marks)

	20X6	20X7
Gross profit margin	40.14%	39.10%
Operating profit margin	14.08%	13.01%
Return on capital employed	13.33%	11.94%
Asset turnover	0.95	0.92
Non-current asset turnover	1.29	1.20
Current ratio	3.86	3.47
Quick ratio	3.11	2.60
Receivables' collection period	39.84 days	46.33 days
Inventory holding in days	45.09 days	53.79 days
Payables' payment period	60.12 days	62.24 days

Note. Total capital employed used ie share capital and reserves + long term loan.

Workings

	20X6	20X7
Gross profit margin	570/1,420	610/1,560
Operating profit margin	200/1,420	203/1,560
Return on capital employed	200/1,500	203/1,700
Asset turnover	1,420/1,500	1,560/1,700
Non-current asset turnover	1,420/1,100	1,560/1,300
Current ratio	540/140	562/162
Quick ratio	435/140	422/162
Receivables' collection period	155/1,420 × 365	198/1,560 × 365
Inventory holding in days	105/850 × 365	140/950 × 365
Payables' payment period	140/850 × 365	162/950 × 365

Note. Total capital employed used ie share capital and reserves + long term loan.

Task 7 (18 marks)

(a)

Product	Units
A	1,000
B	800
C	466

Workings

1 **Determine the limiting factor**

Material usage per unit of each product:

A £9/£3 = 3 kg per unit
B £6/£3 = 2 kg per unit
C £12/£3 = 4 kg per unit

So maximum sales demand would use:

A   3 kg × 1,000 = 3,000 kg
B   2 kg × 800 = 1,600 kg
C   4 kg × 600 = 2,400 kg

Therefore total materials usage for this demand = 3,000 + 1,600 + 2,400 = 7,000 kg

8,000 kg are available so material is not the limiting factor

Labour hours per unit of each product:

A   £6/£12 = 0.5 hours per unit
B   £12/£12 = 1 hour per unit
C   £18/£12 = 1.5 hours per unit

So maximum sales demand would require:

A   0.5 × 1,000 = 500 hours
B   1 × 800 = 800 hours
C   1.5 × 600 = 900 hours

Therefore, total labour hours for this demand = 500 + 800 + 900 = 2,200 hours

Only 2,000 hours are available so labour hours is a limiting factor.

2   **Contribution per limiting factor**

A   (£20 − £9 − £6)/0.5 = £10 per labour hour
B   (£30 − £12 − £6)/1 = £12 per labour hour
C   (£40 − £12 − £18)/1.5 = £6.67 per labour hour

Therefore, rank B, A and then C.

3   **Production to maximise contribution**

B   800 units use 800 hours

A   1,000 units use 500 hours, so 1,300 hours used so far

C   Remaining 2,000 − 1,300 = 700 hours can be used for product C. Makes 700/1.5 = 466 units.

(b)   Labour shortages could be dealt with by employing additional staff. Staff could be temporary if the shortage is not expected to last very long.

A new supplier could be sought in order to deal with any materials shortage. The quality and the cost of using the new supplier would have to be considered.

Material and labour problems could be dealt with by subcontracting some of the production if there is a company capable of producing similar units.

Task 8 (15 marks)

(a) Under traditional costing methods the costs of a product are only recorded and analysed once production of the product has begun. However, it is recognised that a large proportion of the costs of a product are incurred before production has started in the early stages of the product lifecycle. Lifecycle costing recognises all of these pre-production costs of the product such as:

- Design costs
- Prototyping
- Programming
- Process design
- Equipment acquisition

The aim of lifecycle costing is to ensure that all the costs of the product are accumulated over the whole of its lifecycle in order to ensure that all costs are covered by revenue from the product.

(b)

	Year					
	0 £000	1 £000	2 £000	3 £000	4 £000	5 £000
Purchase price	300					
Running cost		30	30	30	30	30
Residual value						(50)
Net cost	300	30	30	30	30	(20)
Discount factor	1.000	0.952	0.907	0.864	0.823	0.784
Present cost	300	28.560	27.210	25.920	24.690	(15.680)

The discounted lifecycle cost of the machine is £ 390,700 .

BPP PRACTICE ASSESSMENT 2
MANAGEMENT ACCOUNTING: DECISION AND CONTROL

Time allowed: 2 hours and 30 minutes

PRACTICE ASSESSMENT 2

Management Accounting: Decision & Control
BPP practice assessment 2

Task 1 (12 marks)

The bagging division of a tea company operates a standard costing system. The standard cost card for the coming months is being prepared and you have been provided with the following information.

- Loose tea is expected to cost £5 per kilogram.

- 1,000 tea bags require 3 kilograms of loose tea.

- Tea bags cost 0.6 pence per bag.

- One machine can package 5,000 bags per hour and requires one operator who costs £10 per hour.

- Budgeted labour hours are 4,000 per month.

- Fixed production overheads are £200,000 per month.

- Budgeted production is 20,000 batches of 1,000 tea bags per month.

- Fixed production overheads are absorbed on the basis of direct labour hours.

Required

(a) Prepare the standard cost card for the production of 1,000 tea bags. (10 marks)

Standard cost card for 1,000 tea bags	£
Direct materials	
Direct materials	
Direct labour	
Fixed overhead	
Total standard cost	

(b) **Calculate the cost of the loose tea for a production level of 1,200 tea bags.** **(2 marks)**

Number of tea bags produced	Total direct materials cost £
1,200	

Task 2 (15 marks)

The standard direct materials cost for a business's product is:

3 kg @ £15 per kg = £45.00

During the last month production was 2,600 units of the product and the actual materials cost was £149,910 for 7,890 kg. The market price of the materials unexpectedly increased by 20% for the whole month.

(a) **Complete the following sentences:** **(9 marks)**

The total materials price variance is £ [   ]

adverse/favourable. The non-controllable element of the materials price

variance that has been caused by the price increase is £ [   ]

adverse/favourable. The controllable element of the materials price

variance caused by other factors is £ [   ]

adverse/favourable.

A business makes one product. Fixed overheads are absorbed on the basis of machine hours. The standard cost card shows that fixed overheads are to be absorbed on the basis of 3 machine hours per unit at a rate of £6 per hour. The budgeted level of production is 10,000 units.

The actual results for the period were that fixed overheads were £192,000, actual machine hours were 29,000 and the actual units produced were 9,500.

(b) **The fixed overhead expenditure variance is:** **(3 marks)**

	✓
£12,000 Favourable	
£12,000 Adverse	
£18,000 Adverse	
£21,000 Adverse	

(c) The fixed overhead volume variance is: **(3 marks)**

	✓
£9,000 Adverse	
£9,000 Favourable	
£6,000 Adverse	
£3,000 Adverse	

Task 3   **(15 marks)**

A business produces a single product in its factory which has two production departments, cutting and finishing. In the following quarter it is anticipated that 200,000 units of the product will be produced. The expected costs are:

Direct materials	£10 per unit
Direct labour	3 hours cutting @ £8.00 per hour
	1 hour finishing @ £9.00 per hour
Variable overheads Cutting	£444,000
Finishing	£382,000
Fixed overheads Cutting	£240,000
Finishing	£110,000

Overheads are absorbed on the basis of direct labour hours.

(a) The absorption cost per unit is: **(2 marks)**

	✓
£45.65	
£46.60	
£47.13	.
£48.88	

(b) **The marginal cost per unit is:** (2 marks)

	✓
£45.65	
£46.60	
£47.13	
£48.88	

A company budgeted to produce 80,000 of its product with a standard cost of £4.60 per unit but in fact produced 84,000 units.

The actual costs of production were:

Materials	278,850
Packaging	8,800
Labour	17,100
Fixed overheads	85,000

The variances for the period have already been calculated:

Materials price	Zero	
Materials usage	£1,650	Adverse
Packaging price	£400	Adverse
Packaging usage	Zero	
Labour rate	£900	Favourable
Labour efficiency	£1,200	Adverse
Fixed overhead expenditure	£5,000	Adverse
Fixed overhead efficiency	£6,000	Adverse
Fixed overhead capacity	£10,000	Favourable

(c) **Calculate the budgeted cost for 84,000 units and then complete the table with the variances to reconcile to the actual cost of production.** **(11 marks)**

			Total £
Budgeted cost for actual production			
Variances	**Favourable £**	**Adverse £**	
Materials price			
Materials usage			
Packaging price			
Packaging usage			
Labour rate			
Labour efficiency			
Fixed overhead expenditure			
Fixed overhead efficiency			
Fixed overhead capacity			
Total variance			
Actual cost of actual production			

Task 4 (12 marks)

Given below are the production cost figures for the last nine months.

(a) **Calculate a three-month moving average for these figures.**

(10 marks)

	Production costs £	Three-month moving total £	Three-month moving average £
March	226,500		
April	245,300		
May	240,800		
June	231,400		
July	237,600		
August	246,000		
September	241,200		
October	242,300		
November	247,500		
December	249,300		

(b) **The three-month moving average represents which of the following?** (2 marks)

Picklist:

Cyclical variations
Random variations
Seasonal variations
Trend

Task 5 (18 marks)

Dickenson plc manufactures a range of products for use in the motor racing industry. The company uses a standard absorption costing system with variances calculated quarterly.

It is midway through quarter three of the current financial year and a number of events have occurred which may impact on the quarter-end variances for a particular product, MTRF1.

The production director has asked for a report indicating the possible effects of the various events.

Production notes for MTRF1

(a)   MTRF1 uses a specialist industry material – POL89.

(b)   Recent advances in the production of POL89 have increased its availability which has led to a reduction in the price per litre by 18% in the last month. It is expected that the reduction in price will remain until at least the end of quarter three.

(c)   The standard price was set before the decrease in price occurred.

(d)   The quality control officer has tested the latest batch of POL89 and reported that it is of a higher quality than expected.

(e)   The company implemented a strict material usage policy at the beginning of quarter three to monitor levels of wastage. This was overseen by the quality control department with no additional payroll costs being incurred.

(f)   Employees usually receive an annual pay rise at the beginning of quarter three and this was included in the standard cost. Due to the current economic climate this pay rise has been suspended indefinitely.

(g)   The budgeted production for the quarter is 12,000 units.

(h)   An order for 3,000 units was cancelled shortly after the beginning of quarter three. The company has been unable to replace this order and the actual production for the quarter is now expected to be 9,000 units. The production machinery needed to be recalibrated to deal with the higher quality POL89. In addition, one of the machines was found to be defective and required a complete overhaul. These costs are to be included in fixed overheads at the end of the quarter.

Required

Complete the report for the Production Director on the possible impact of the above events on the POL89 price and usage variances, direct labour rate and efficiency variances and the fixed overhead expenditure and volume variances. The report should:

- **Identify whether each variance is likely to be adverse or favourable at the end of the quarter**

- **Explain what each variance means**

- **Provide one possible reason why each variance is likely to be adverse or favourable at the end of the quarter**
- **Identify possible links between the variances**

You are NOT required to make any calculations.

To: Production Director	**Subject:** Analysis of variances
From: Accounts Technician	**Date:** XX/XX/20XX

POL89 price variance

POL89 usage variance

Direct labour efficiency variance

Fixed overhead expenditure variance

Fixed overhead volume variance

Task 6 (15 marks)

Voltair Ltd has developed a domestic wind turbine. A colleague has prepared forecast information based upon two scenarios. The forecast statements of profit or loss (income statements) and statements of financial position for both scenarios are shown below.

- Scenario 1 is to set the price at £1,250 per unit with sales of 10,000 units each year.

- Scenario 2 is to set the price at £1,000 per unit with sales of 14,000 units each year.

Forecast statement of profit or loss (income statement)

	Scenario 1 £000	Scenario 2 £000
Revenue	12,500	14,000
Cost of production		
Direct (raw) materials	3,000	4,200
Direct labour	2,000	2,800
Fixed production overheads	3,000	3,000
Total cost of sales	8,000	10,000
Gross profit	4,500	4,000
Selling and distribution costs	1,000	1,000
Administration costs	750	750
Operating profit	2,750	2,250
Interest payable	600	600
Net profit	2,150	1,650

Extracts from the forecast statement of financial position

	£000	£000
Non-current assets	20,000	20,000
Current assets	5,000	5,500
Current liabilities	4,600	5,800
Long-term loans	12,000	11,300
	8,400	8,400
Represented by:		
Share capital	5,650	6,150
Reserves	2,750	2,250
	8,400	8,400

(a) Calculate the following performance indicators for each scenario. Give your answer to TWO decimal places:

(9 marks)

(i) **Gross profit margin**
(ii) **Net profit margin**
(iii) **Direct materials cost per unit**
(iv) **Direct labour cost per unit**
(v) **Fixed production cost per unit**
(vi) **Gearing ratio**
(vii) **Interest cover**

A business sells a single product and has budgeted sales of 130,000 units for the next period. The selling price per unit is £56 and the variable costs of production are £36. The fixed costs of the business are £2,000,000.

(b) Complete the following sentences. Give your answers to the nearest whole number. **(6 marks)**

The breakeven point in units is ⬚ units.

The margin of safety in units is ⬚ units.

The margin of safety as a percentage of budgeted sales is ⬚ %.

Task 7 (18 marks)

(a) **What is a limiting factor and why is it important?** **(5 marks)**

(b) **Give three examples of possible limiting factors for a manufacturing organisation other than sales demand.**

(3 marks)

A company makes two products, the Daisy and the Rose. The information below relates to June, when materials will be limited to 52,000 kg and labour hours will be limited to 25,000 hours.

Per unit	Daisy £	Rose £
Direct materials at £4 per kg	12	16
Direct labour at £10 per hour	20	10
Variable overheads	10	5
Selling price	50	46

Per unit	Daisy £ Units	Rose £ Units
Sales demand	6,000	10,000

(c) **Complete the table below for June.** **(7 marks)**

	Daisy	Rose
Contribution per unit (£)		
Contribution per limiting factor (£) (to TWO decimal places)		
Optimal production (units)		

The total fixed costs for June are expected to be £100,000.

(d) **Calculate the maximum profit resulting from the optimal production plan.** **(3 marks)**

£	

....

Task 8 **(15 marks)**

A company is reviewing various alternatives to determine whether it is possible to reduce monthly costs. The operations director is considering whether to invest in a new machine which:

- Could either be purchased for £3 million or rented for £50,000 per month
- Is expected to have a life of 10 years and a scrap value of £900,000

It is assumed under both options that:

- The maintenance cost of the machine is £50,000 per annum
- Decommissioning costs will be £100,000
- The machine will be used for 10 years

Required

(a) **Calculate the lifecycle cost of the TWO options outlined.**

Ignore the time value of money and any opportunity costs when calculating the lifecycle cost. **(12 marks)**

Renting the machine

Calculations:

Buying the machine

Calculations:

(b) Explain target costing and how to calculate target cost.

(3 marks)

BPP PRACTICE ASSESSMENT 2
MANAGEMENT ACCOUNTING:
DECISION AND CONTROL

ANSWERS

Management Accounting: Decision & Control
BPP practice assessment 2

Task 1 (12 marks)

(a)

Standard cost card for 1,000 tea bags	£
Direct materials – tea (3kg × £5)	15.00
Direct materials – bags (1,000 × £0.006)	6.00
Direct labour $\left(\dfrac{1,000}{5,000 \text{ hours}} \times £10 \right)$	2.00
Fixed overhead $\left(\dfrac{0.2 \text{ hours} \times £200,000}{4,000 \text{ hours}} \right)$	10.00
Total standard cost	33.00

(b)

Number of tea bags produced	Total direct materials cost £
1,200	18.00

1,000 tea bags require 3 kgs of loose tea, therefore 1,200 tea bags will require 3 kgs × 1.2 = 3.6 kg.

Cost of tea = 3.6 kg × £5 = £18.

Task 2 (15 marks)

(a) The total materials price variance is £ | £31,560 | adverse.

The non-controllable element of the materials price variance that has been caused by the price increase is £ | 23,670 | adverse.

The controllable element of the materials price variance caused by other factors is £ | 7,890 | adverse.

Workings

1 **Total materials price variance**

	£
7,890 should have cost (× £15)	118,350
But did cost	149,910
	31,560 (A)

2 **Non-controllable variance caused by price increase**

	£
Standard cost for actual quantity 7,890 × £15	118,350
Adjusted cost for actual quantity 7,890 × £18*	142,020
	23,670 (A)

*Adjusted price is 120% of £15 = £18

3 **Controllable variance caused by other factors**

	£
Adjusted cost for actual quantity 7,890 × £18	142,020
Actual cost	149,910
	7,890 (A)

(b)

	✓
£12,000 Favourable	
£12,000 Adverse	✓
£18,000 Adverse	
£21,000 Adverse	

(c)

	✓
£9,000 Adverse	✓
£9,000 Favourable	
£6,000 Adverse	
£3,000 Adverse	

Workings

1 Fixed overhead expenditure variance

	£
Budgeted fixed overhead 10,000 units × 3 hours × £6	180,000
Actual fixed overhead	192,000
Expenditure variance	12,000 (A)

2 Fixed overhead volume variance

	£
Standard hours for actual production @ standard OAR 9,500 units × 3 hours × £6	171,000
Standard hours for budgeted production @ standard OAR 10,000 units × 3 hours × £6	180,000
Volume variance	9,000 (A)

Task 3 (15 marks)

(a)

	✓
£45.65	
£46.60	
£47.13	
£48.88	✓

(b)

	✓
£45.65	
£46.60	
£47.13	✓
£48.88	

Workings

1   **Absorption costing**

	£
Direct materials	10.00
Direct labour – Cutting (3 × £8.00)	24.00
– Finishing	9.00
Variable overheads:	
Cutting (£444,000/600,000) × 3 hrs	2.22
Finishing (£382,000/200,000) × 1hr	1.91
Fixed overheads:	
Cutting (£240,000/600,000) × 3 hrs	1.20
Finishing (£110,000/200,000) × 1 hr	0.55
	48.88

2   **Marginal costing**

	£
Direct materials	10.00
Direct labour – Cutting (3 × £8.00)	24.00
– Finishing	9.00
Variable overheads:	
Cutting (£440,000/600,000) × 3 hrs	2.22
Finishing (£382,000/200,000) × 1 hr	1.91
	47.13

	Favourable £	Adverse £	Total £
Budgeted cost for actual production (84,000 × £4.60)			**386,400**
Variances	**Favourable £**	**Adverse £**	
Materials price	–	–	
Materials usage		1,650	
Packaging price		400	
Packaging usage	–	–	
Labour rate	900		
Labour efficiency		1,200	
Fixed overhead expenditure		5,000	
Fixed overhead efficiency		6,000	
Fixed overhead capacity	10,000		
Total variance	10,900	14,250	3,350
Actual cost of actual production (£278,850 + £8,800 + £17,100 + £85,000)			389,750

Task 4 (12 marks)

(a)

	Production costs £	Three-month moving total £	Three-month moving average £
March	226,500		
April	245,300	712,600	237,533
May	240,800	717,500	239,167
June	231,400	709,800	236,600
July	237,600	715,000	238,333
August	246,000	724,800	241,600
September	241,200	729,500	243,167
October	242,300	731,000	243,667
November	247,500	739,100	246,367
December	249,300		

(b) The correct answer is: | Trend |

....

Task 5 (18 marks)

POL89 price variance

The POL89 price variance is likely to be favourable.

This is due to a reduction in price of 18% during the quarter, resulting in the actual price being lower than the standard price.

POL89 usage variance

The POL89 usage variance is likely to be favourable.

The purchase of a higher quality product would usually be expected to result in less wastage, and therefore the actual quantity used would be lower than the standard usage.

The usage and price variances are often linked when a higher priced and therefore higher quality product may reduce wastage costs, however in this case the higher quality is probably due to the advances in production of POL89 and so is unlikely to be linked with the POL89 price variance.

Employees may be demotivated from the lack of pay rise but the new material usage control policy recently implemented should keep material usage favourable.

Direct labour efficiency variance

The direct labour efficiency variance is likely to be adverse, with each unit taking more hours to manufacture than expected.

Efficiency will be affected by the demotivational effects of the suspension of the pay rise.

In addition, the cancelled order means that production will be lower by 25% during the quarter and there is likely to be idle time for employees which will have an adverse effect on the labour efficiency.

Fixed overhead expenditure variance

The fixed overhead expenditure variance is likely to be adverse, due to costs of recalibrating the machines and the repair of the defective machine. Therefore the actual fixed overheads will be higher than expected.

Fixed overhead volume variance

The fixed overhead volume variance is likely to be adverse because the actual volume produced is likely to be 25% lower than the forecast volume due to the cancellation of the order for 3,000 units. Therefore overheads are likely to be under-absorbed.

Task 6 (15 marks)

(a)

		Scenario 1	Scenario 2
(i)	Gross profit margin		
	= Gross Profit/ Revenue (turnover) × 100	(4,500/12,500) × 100 = 36.00%	(4,000/14,000) × 100 = 28.57%
(ii)	Net profit margin		
	= Net Profit/ Revenue × 100	(2,150/12,500) × 100 = 17.20%	(1,650/14,000) × 100 = 11.79%
(iii)	Direct materials cost per unit		
	= Direct materials cost/Sales units	£3,000,000/10,000 = £300.00	£4,200,000/14,000 = £300.00
(iv)	Direct labour cost per unit		
	= Direct labour cost/Sales units	£2,000,000/10,000 = £200.00	£2,800,000/14,000 = £200.00
(v)	Fixed production cost per unit		
	= Fixed production cost/ Sales units	£3,000,000/10,000 = £300.00	£3,000,000/14,000 = £214.29

	Scenario 1	Scenario 2
(vi) Gearing		
= Total debt/ (Total debt + Share capital + Reserves)	12,000/(12,000 + 8,400) = (0.59 or 58.82%)	11,300/(11,300 + 8,400) = 0.57 or 57.36%
Alternative answer for gearing:		
Gearing		
= Total debt/ (Share capital + Reserves)	12,000/8,400 = (1.43 or 142.86%)	11,300/8,400 = (1.35 or 134.52%)
(vii) Interest cover		
= Operating profit /Interest payable	2,750/600 = 4.58	2,250/600 = 3.75

(b) The breakeven point in units is $\boxed{100,000}$ units.

The margin of safety in units is $\boxed{30,000}$ units.

The margin of safety as a percentage of budgeted sales is $\boxed{23}$ %.

Workings

1 **Breakeven point** $= \dfrac{£2,000,000}{£56 - £36} \times 100\%$

$= 100,000$ units

2 **Margin of safety (units)** = Budgeted sales – breakeven sales

$= (130,000 - 100,000)$ units

$= 30,000$ units

3 **Margin of safety (% budgeted sales)**

$= \dfrac{130,000 - 100,000}{130,000} \times 100\%$

$= 23\%$

Task 7 (18 marks)

(a) The limiting factor (or scarce resource) is the element or resource of the business that is likely to be the one that places limitations on the activities of the business. It is unlikely in a business that it will be able to produce and sell an unlimited number of its products. There will normally be one factor, at least, that will limit the quantity of sales and/or production. The limiting factor is important because of the effect it has on production planning. The plans of the business must be built around the limiting factor. For example, an optimal production plan is formed to make the most profitable use of the limiting factor.

The most common limiting factor is that of sales demand. Therefore the sales forecast must be made first and the production budget will then be based upon the forecast sales levels.

(b) Any three of the following:

- Limitations on the amount of raw materials that can be purchased

- Manpower limitations – a limit to the number of hours that can be worked in the period by the labour force

- Capacity limitations – a limit to the number of machine hours available

- A limit to the quantity that can be produced by a production line in the period

(c)

	Daisy	Rose
Contribution per unit (£) (W1)	8	15
Contribution per limiting factor (£) (to TWO decimal places) (W2)	2.67	3.75
Optimal production (units)	4,000	10,000

Workings

1   Contribution per unit

Contribution = selling price – variable costs
Daisy: £50 – £12 – £20 – £10 = £8
Rose: £46 – £16 – £10 – £5 = £15

2 **Contribution per limiting factor**

Establish limiting factor

Total material required = (6,000 units × 3kg) + (10,000 units × 4kg) = 58,000 kg therefore material is a limiting factor.

Total labour required = (6,000 units × 2 hours) + (10,000 units × 1 hour) = 22,000 hours therefore labour is not a limiting factor.

Contribution per limiting factor:

Daisy £8/3kg = 2.67
Rose £15/4 kg = 3.75

3 **Optimal production**

Optimal production plan is to produce maximum demand for Rose first.

10,000 units × 4 kg = 40,000 kg leaving 12,000 kg to make Daisy.

Number of units of Daisy = 12,000 kg / 3 =4,000 units

(d) £82,000

Total profit = Contribution – fixed costs = [(4,000 × £8) + (10,000 × £15)] – £100,000 = £82,000

Task 8 (15 marks)

(a) Lifecycle costs of renting the machine

	£
Rental (£50,000 × 12 months × 10 years)	6,000,000
Maintenance (£50,000 × 10 years)	500,000
Decommissioning	100,000
Total	6,600,000

Lifecycle costs of buying the machine

	£
Purchase	3,000,000
Maintenance (£50,000 × 10 years)	500,000
Decommissioning	100,000
Scrap value	(900,000)
Total	2,700,000

(b) Target costing is a method used to achieve a required profit in circumstances where the company has to take a given market price for its product.

Target costing involves setting a target cost by subtracting a desired profit margin from a competitive market price. A target cost is the maximum amount of cost that can be incurred on a product and with it the firm can still earn the required profit margin from that product at a particular selling price.

Selling price – required profit = target cost

BPP PRACTICE ASSESSMENT 3
MANAGEMENT ACCOUNTING: DECISION AND CONTROL

Time allowed: 2 hours and 30 minutes

Management Accounting: Decision & Control
BPP practice assessment 3

Task 1 (12 marks)

A business produces one product which requires the following inputs:

Direct materials	3 kg @ £6.20 per kg
Direct labour	7 hours @ £8.00 per hour
Rent/rates	£24,000 per quarter
Leased delivery vans	£1,000 for every 900 units of production
Warehouse costs	£10,000 per quarter plus £2.00 per unit

Complete the table to show the total cost of production and the cost per unit at each of the quarterly production levels. Show the cost per unit to TWO decimal places (dp). **(12 marks)**

Production level Units	Total cost of production £	Cost per unit £
2,000		
3,000		
4,000		

Task 2 (15 marks)

A company purchases 14,000 kg of material at a cost of £58,000. The standard cost per kg is £4.

(a) **The total materials price variance is:** **(3 marks)**

	✓
£14,000	
£2,000	
£58,000	
£4.14	

The variance is [▼]

Picklist:

adverse
favourable

A company purchases 10,000 kg of material at a cost of £22,000. The budgeted production was 6,000 units which requires 9,000 kg of material at a total standard cost of £18,000. The actual production was 6,500 units.

(b) **The material usage variance is:** (3 marks)

	✓
500 kg	
250 kg	
£500	
£250	

The variance is [▼] .

Picklist:

adverse
favourable

Extracts from Drizzle Co's records from last period are as follows:

	Budget	Actual
Production	1,925 units	2,070 units
Variable production overhead cost	£13,475	£13,455
Labour hours worked	3,850	2,990

(c) **The variable production overhead expenditure variance for the last period is** £ [ ] . (2 marks)

The variance is [▼] . (1 mark)

Picklist:

adverse
favourable

A company reported a favourable variance of £5,000 for fixed overhead expenditure in June. The budgeted fixed overhead expenditure variance for June was £120,000.

(d)   What was the actual fixed overhead expenditure in June?

(3 marks)

£ [   ]

A company reported an adverse variance of £12,000 for fixed overhead volume in July. Budgeted production was 20,000 units and the standard fixed overhead cost per unit was £6

(e)   What was the actual number of units produced in July?

(3 marks)

[   ] units

··

Task 3 (15 marks)

The budgeted activity and actual results for a business for the month of May 20X8 are as follows:

		Budget		Actual
Production (tonnes)		200		210
Direct labour	600 hours	£4,800	600 hours	£5,100
Fixed overheads		£90,000		£95,000

(a)   Complete the table to calculate the following: (7 marks)

	£
Budgeted overhead absorption rate per tonne	
Overheads absorbed into actual production	
Fixed overhead expenditure variance	
Fixed overhead volume variance	

The standard labour cost for one unit of product Z is £24 (3 hours @ £8 per hour). The budgeted level of production is 14,000 units.

Actual results for the period are:

Production   13,200 units
Labour   18,600 hours costing £111,600

BPP
LEARNING MEDIA

369

(b) **Prepare a reconciliation of the budgeted labour cost with the actual labour cost using the labour cost variances.** **(6 marks)**

			Total £
Standard cost of labour for actual production			
Variances	**Favourable £**	**Adverse £**	
Direct labour rate variance			
Direct labour efficiency variance			
Total variance			
Actual cost of labour for actual production			

(c) **Which fixed overhead variances would be included in an operating statement prepared under a system of marginal costing?** **(2 marks)**

	✓
Fixed overhead volume variance only	
Fixed overhead expenditure variance and fixed overhead volume variance	
Fixed overhead expenditure variance only	

··

Task 4 (12 marks)

A material which is derived from soft fruit is either imported or purchased from UK farmers by a company. The price of the material fluctuates month by month depending on the time of year. The cost information for the four months ending August 20X6 is given below.

	May 20X6 £	June 20X6 £	July 20X6 £	August 20X6 £
Cost per 1,000 kg	1,000	900	700	800

The underlying cost does not change during the period May to August. The change in cost over the four months is due only to the seasonal variations which are given below.

| | May 20X6 | June 20X6 | July 20X6 | August 20X6 |
	£	£	£	£
Seasonal variations	200	100	−100	0

(a) **Complete the table to calculate the underlying cost per 1,000 kilograms for the period May to August 20X6.** **(5 marks)**

	May 20X6 £	June 20X6 £	July 20X6 £	Aug 20X6 £
Cost per 1,000 kg				
Seasonal variation				
Trend				

Indications are that the underlying cost per 1,000 kilograms for the period May 20X7 to August 20X7 will be £850.

(b) **The percentage increase in the underlying cost from 20X6 to 20X7 is** ⬚ **% (to 2 dp).** **(2 marks)**

(c) **Complete the table to calculate the forecast cost per 1,000 kilograms for the period May 20X7 to August 20X7 using the underlying cost and the seasonal variations given above.**
(5 marks)

	May 20X7 £	June 20X7 £	July 20X7 £	Aug 20X7 £
Trend				
Seasonal variation				
Cost per 1,000 kg				

Task 5 (18 marks)

Given below is the operating statement for a manufacturing business for the last month:

Reconciliation of standard cost of actual production to actual cost – March 20X9

| | Variances | | |
	Favourable £	Adverse £	£
Standard cost of actual production			672,500
Variances			
Materials price		24,300	
Materials usage	6,780		
Labour rate		10,600	
Labour efficiency	10,300		
Fixed overhead expenditure	7,490		
Fixed overhead volume (favourable efficiency and capacity variances)	10,900		
	35,470	34,900	(570)
Actual cost of production			671,930

A number of factors about the month's production have been discovered:

- At the end of the previous month a new warehouse had been purchased which has meant a saving in warehouse rental.

- Six new machines were installed at the start of the month which are more power efficient than the old machines, but also more expensive, causing a larger depreciation charge.

- There was an unexpected increase in the materials price during the month and when other suppliers were contacted it was found that they were all charging approximately the same price for the materials.

- A higher than normal skilled grade of labour was used during the month due to staff shortages. The production process is a skilled process and the benefit has been that these employees, although more expensive, have produced the goods faster and with less wastage. This particular group of employees are also keen to work overtime and, as the business wishes to build up inventory levels, advantage of this has been taken.

Required

Prepare a report for the production director.

Your report should do the following:

(a) **Suggest what effect the combination of the factors given above might have had on the reported variances.**

(b) **Make suggestions as to any action that should be taken in light of these factors.**

REPORT

To: Production Director
From: Management Accountant
Date: xx/xx/xx
Subject: March 20X9 variances

New warehouse

New machines

Price increase

Skilled labour

Task 6 (15 marks)

Given below is the statement of profit or loss (income statement) for a business for the year ending 31 March 20X9 and a statement of financial position at that date.

Statement of profit or loss (income statement)

	£	£
Revenue		2,650,400
Cost of sales		
Opening inventory	180,000	
Purchases	1,654,400	
	1,834,400	
Less closing inventory	191,200	
		1,643,200
Gross profit		1,007,200
Less expenses		
Selling and distribution costs	328,400	
Administration expenses	342,200	
		670,600
Operating profit		336,600
Interest payable		36,000
Profit after interest		300,600

Statement of financial position

	£	£
Non-current assets		1,920,400
Current assets		
Inventory	191,200	
Receivables	399,400	
Bank	16,800	
	607,400	
Payables	(190,300)	
Net current assets		417,100
		2,337,500
Less long term loan		600,000
		1,737,500
Share capital		1,000,000
Other reserves		150,000
Retained earnings		587,500
		1,737,500

(a) **Using the statement of profit or loss (income statement) and statement of financial position complete the table to calculate the performance indicators. Give your answer to TWO dp (unless otherwise stated).** **(12 marks)**

Gross profit margin	
Operating profit margin	
Return on capital employed	
Asset turnover	
Current ratio	
Receivables' collection period (to the nearest whole number)	
Payables' payment period (to the nearest whole number)	

(b) **If the payables' payment period was increased to 60 days what effect would this have on the cash balance? Give your answer to the nearest whole £.** **(3 marks)**

£

....

Task 7 **(18 marks)**

Jay Ltd manufactures three products, Product Kay, Product Elle and Product Emm. In June there will be a shortage of labour due to staff holidays and only 1,800 hours will be available.

The following information relates to June:

Per unit	Product Kay £	Product Elle £	Product Emm £
Variable production cost	7.00	2.50	5.00
Selling price	13.00	10.00	11.00
Sales demand (units)	300	600	400
Labour hours required to meet maximum sales demand (hrs)	600	900	1,200

(a) **Complete the table to show the optimal production plan using the available labour hours. Show all figures to two decimal places.** **(8 marks)**

	Product Kay	Product Elle	Product Emm
Labour hours required per unit			
Contribution per unit (£)			
Contribution per limiting factor (£)			
Optimal production plan (units)			

(b) **Calculate the total contribution from Product Emm if the optimal production plan is used.** **(3 marks)**

£

(c)   **Explain the following.**   **(8 marks)**

  (i)   **How to decide whether a resource is a limiting factor**

  (ii)   **How you would calculate the extra resource required to meet demand**

How to decide whether a resource is a limiting factor

How to calculate the extra resource required to meet demand

Task 8   **(15 marks)**

The costs of the maintenance department of a manufacturing business are estimated to be £102,000 for the following quarter. During that period it is estimated that there will be 50 maintenance visits on site. Product X will require 10 maintenance visits during the quarter and Product Y 40 maintenance visits.

(a) **Complete the table below using activity based costing to show how much maintenance overhead will be absorbed into Product X and Product Y.** (4 marks)

	£
Overhead included in Product X	
Overhead included in Product Y	

A manufacturer, operating in a competitive market, can sell its product at £35 per unit. It wishes to make a profit margin of 40%. Each unit of product requires 1 hour of labour at £6/hour and incurs other overheads at a rate of £7/labour hour. The product requires 4 kg of material per unit.

(b) **What is the maximum that the manufacturer can afford to pay for each kg of material?** (6 marks)

Maximum £ per kg: £

(c) **Explain the term lifecycle costing and why discounted cash flow techniques should be used in a lifecycle costing analysis.** (5 marks)

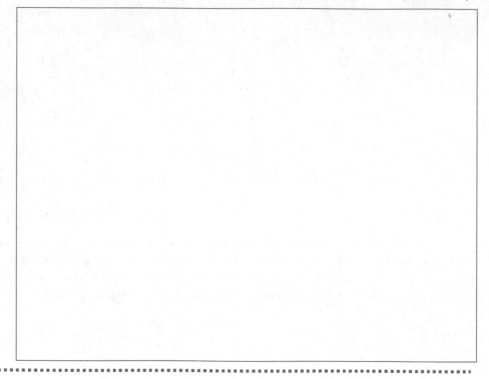

BPP PRACTICE ASSESSMENT 3
MANAGEMENT ACCOUNTING:
DECISION AND CONTROL

ANSWERS

Management Accounting: Decision & Control
BPP practice assessment 3

Task 1

Production level Units	Total cost of production £	Cost per unit £
2,000	190,200	95.10
3,000	267,800	89.27
4,000	345,400	86.35

Workings

	2,000 units £	3,000 units £	4,000 units £
Direct materials 3kg × £6.20 × units	37,200	55,800	74,400
Direct labour 7 hours × £8.00 × units	112,000	168,000	224,000
Rent/rates	24,000	24,000	24,000
Leased delivery vans	3,000	4,000	5,000
Warehouse costs £10,000 + £2.00 × units	14,000	16,000	18,000
	190,200	267,800	345,400
Cost per unit	£95.10	£89.27	£86.35

Task 2

(a)

	✓
£14,000	
£2,000	✓
£58,000	
£4.14	

The variance is [adverse] .

Working:

	£
14,000 kg should have cost (× £4)	56,000
But did cost	58,000
Total materials price variance	2,000 (A)

(b)

	✓
500 kg	
250 kg	
£500	✓
£250	

The variance is [adverse] .

Working:

6,500 units should have used × 1.5 kg	9,750 kg
But did use	10,000 kg
	250 kg
@ Standard rate per kg £2	× £2
Materials usage variance	£500 (A)

(c) | £ | 2,990 | | adverse |

Workings

Standard variable production overhead cost per hour = £13,475/3850 = £3.50

	£
2,990 hours of variable production overhead should cost (× £3.50)	10,465
But did cost	13,455
Variable production overhead expenditure variance	2,990 (A)

(d) £115,000

Workings

	£
Budgeted fixed overhead	120,000
Actual fixed overhead (balancing figure)	115,000
Fixed overhead expenditure variance	5,000 (F)

(e) 18,000 units

Workings

Variance in units = £12,000/£6 = 2,000

Actual production = 20,000 – 2,000 = 18,000 units

Alternatively:

	Units
Actual production (balancing figure)	18,000
Budgeted production	20,000
Fixed overhead volume variance in units	2,000 (A)
Standard fixed overhead cost per unit	£6
Fixed overhead volume variance in £	12,000 (A)

Task 3

(a)

	£
Budgeted overhead absorption rate per tonne	450
Overheads absorbed into actual production	94,500
Fixed overhead expenditure variance	5,000 Adverse
Fixed overhead volume variance	4,500 Favourable

Workings

Budgeted overhead absorption rate per tonne = Fixed overheads/Budgeted output

= £90,000/200 tonnes

= £450

Overheads absorbed into actual production = Actual production × Absorption rate

= 210 units × £450

= £94,500

1   Fixed overhead expenditure variance

	£
Budgeted fixed overhead	90,000
Actual fixed overhead	95,000
Fixed overhead expenditure variance	5,000 Adv

2   Fixed overhead volume variance

	£
Actual production at absorption rate per unit (210 × £450)	94,500
Budgeted production at absorption rate per unit	90,000
Fixed overhead volume variance	4,500 Fav

(b)

			Total £
Standard cost of labour for actual production			316,800
Variances	**Favourable £**	**Adverse £**	
Direct labour rate variance	37,200		
Direct labour efficiency variance	168,000		
Total variance			(205,200)
Actual cost of labour for actual production			111,600

Working:

Standard cost for actual units produced = 13,200 units × 3hrs × £8 = £316,800

Labour rate variance	£
18,600 hrs should have cost (× £8)	148,800
But did cost	111,600
Rate variance	37,200 (F)

Labour efficiency variance	
13,200 units should have taken (× 3 hours)	39,600 hrs
But did take	18,600 hrs
	21,000 (F)
At standard cost	× £8
Usage variance	168,000 (F)

(c)

	✓
Fixed overhead volume variance only	
Fixed overhead expenditure variance and fixed overhead volume variance	
Fixed overhead expenditure variance only	✓

Task 4

(a)

	May 20X6 £	June 20X6 £	July 20X6 £	Aug 20X6 £
Cost per 1,000 kgs	1,000	900	700	800
Seasonal variation	200	100	(100)	0
Trend	800	800	800	800

Note. The underlying cost is the trend.

(b) The percentage increase in the underlying cost from 20X6 to 20X7 is 6.25%

$$\left(\frac{(850 - 800)}{800} \right) \times 100 = \boxed{6.25\%}$$

Note. The above calculation is the most normal way of calculating a change from one period to the next, as a percentage of the original figure.

(c)

	May 20X7 £	June 20X7 £	July 20X7 £	Aug 20X7 £
Trend	850	850	850	850
Seasonal variation	200	100	(100)	0
Cost per 1,000 kgs	1,050	950	750	850

Task 5

REPORT

To: Production Director
From: Management Accountant
Date: xx/xx/xx
Subject: March 20X9 variances

New warehouse

This will have the effect of simply reducing the fixed overhead expense (assuming the rent saved exceeds any new depreciation charge) and therefore is part of the favourable fixed overhead expenditure variance. The standard fixed overhead cost should be adjusted to reflect the rental saving.

New machines

The new machines use less power than the old ones therefore reducing the power costs element of the fixed overhead. The additional depreciation charge however will increase the fixed overhead expense. Once the reduction in power costs and increase in depreciation charge are known then the standard fixed overhead should be adjusted.

Price increase

The price increase will be a cause of the adverse materials price variance. The price increase appears to be a permanent one as all suppliers have increased their prices, so the standard materials cost should be altered.

Skilled labour

The use of the higher skilled labour will have been part of the cause of the favourable labour efficiency variance and the favourable materials usage variance. If the fixed overheads are absorbed on a labour hour basis then the efficiency of the skilled labour will also be a cause of a favourable fixed overhead efficiency variance. The additional expense of the skilled labour and the overtime that has been worked will have been causes of the adverse labour rate variance. The overtime may also have led to a favourable capacity variance as actual hours exceeded the budgeted hours. Unless the use of this grade of labour is likely to be a permanent policy, then there should be no change to the standard labour rate or hours.

Task 6

(a)

Gross profit margin	38.00%
Operating profit margin	12.70%
Return on capital employed	14.40%
Asset turnover	1.13
Current ratio	3.19
Receivables' collection period	55 days
Payables' payment period	42 days

Workings

1 **Gross profit margin**

$$= \frac{\text{Gross profit}}{\text{Revenue}} \times 100$$

$$= \frac{1,007,200}{2,650,400} \times 100$$

$$= 38.00\%$$

2 **Operating profit margin**

$$= \frac{\text{Operating profit}}{\text{Revenue}} \times 100$$

$$= \frac{336,600}{2,650,400} \times 100$$

$$= 12.70\%$$

3 **Return on capital employed**

$$= \frac{\text{Operating profit}}{\text{Non - current assets} + \text{Net current assets}} \times 1$$

$$= \frac{336,600}{2,337,500} \times 100$$

$$= 14.40\%$$

4 **Asset turnover**

$$= \frac{\text{Revenue}}{\text{Capital employed}}$$

$$= \frac{2,650,400}{2,337,500}$$

$$= 1.13$$

5   **Current ratio** $= \dfrac{\text{Current assets}}{\text{Current liabilities}}$

$$= \dfrac{607,400}{190,300}$$

$$= 3.19$$

6   **Receivables' collection period** $= \dfrac{\text{Receivables}}{\text{Revenue}} \times 365$

$$= \dfrac{399,400}{2,650,400} \times 365$$

$$= 55 \text{ days}$$

7   **Payables' payment period** $= \dfrac{\text{Payables}}{\text{Purchases}} \times 365$

$$= \dfrac{190,300}{1,654,400} \times 365$$

$$= 42 \text{ days}$$

(b)   Increase in cash balance $= \dfrac{£1,654,400}{365} \times (60 - 42)$

$$= \boxed{£ \quad 81,587}$$

Task 7

(a)

	Product Kay	Product Elle	Product Emm
Labour hours required per unit (W1)	2.00	1.50	3.00
Contribution per unit (£) (W2)	6.00	7.50	6.00
Contribution per limiting factor (£) (W3)	3.00	5.00	2.00
Optimal production plan (units) (W4)	300	600	100

Workings

1 **Labour hours required per unit**

Labour hours required per unit = Labour hrs required to meet demand / sales demand units

Product Kay: 600/300 = 2 hours per unit

Product Elle: 900/600 = 1.5 hours per unit

Product Emm: 1,200/400 = 3 hours per unit

2 **Contribution per unit**

Contribution per unit = selling price – variable production cost

Product Kay: = 13.00 – 7.00 = £6.00 per unit

Product Elle: = 10.00 – 2.50 = £7.50 per unit

Product Emm: = £11.00 - £5.00 = £6.00 per unit

3 **Contribution per limiting factor**

Contribution per limiting factor = Contribution/labour hours required

Product Kay: = £6.00/2 hrs = £3.00 per unit

Product Elle: = £7.50/1.5 hrs = £5.00 per unit

Product Emm: = £6.00/3 hrs = £2.00 per unit

Therefore ranking is (1) Elle, (2) Kay, (3) Emm.

4 **Optimal production plan**

If we meet full demand for Elle and Kay, we will use 900 + 600 = 1,500 hours. This leaves 1,800 – 1,500 = 300 hours to use on Emm. Number of units of Emm we can make from 300 hours = 300/3 hrs = 100 units

(b) | £ | 600 |

100 units × £6.00 = £600

(c) How to decide whether a resource is a limiting factor

The way to work out whether there is a scarce resource is to calculate the total amount of each resource required to meet maximum demand.

For example, the total required number of labour hours in part (a) to meet sales demand is 600 + 900 + 1,200 = 2,700 hours. As there were only 1,800 hours available, labour hours are a scarce resource.

How to calculate the extra resource required to meet demand

The extra resource required to meet demand is the difference between the total amount required and the total amount available.

For example, the extra resource required for meet demand in part (a) = 2,700 hours – 1,800 hours = 900 hours.

....

Task 8

(a)

	£
Overhead included in Product X	20,400
Overhead included in Product Y	81,600

Working:

Maintenance cost per visit	=	£102,000/50	=	£2,040
Product X	=	10 × £2,040	=	£20,400
Product Y	=	40 × £2,040	=	£81,600

(b) Maximum £ per kg = £ 2.00

	Working £
Selling price	35.00
40% margin	14.00
Target cost	21.00
Less	
Labour 1 hr @ £6/hr	(6.00)
Overheads 1 hr @ £7/hr	(7.00)
Available for 4kg material	8.00
Maximum price per kg	2.00

(c) Lifecycle costing is an accounting technique whereby the cost of an activity, project or piece of machinery is considered and calculated over the whole of its economic life, from purchase through to eventual disposal. Therefore the initial cost of investment is only part of the cost of the project and other costs will include operating costs and revenues, maintenance costs, decommissioning costs and final residual value.

In a lifecycle costing analysis the cash flows relating to the project are considered over its entire life which may spread over many years. As with any project being considered where cash flows in the future are being assessed, the time value of money must be considered. Therefore, to find the true cost of the cash flows associated with the project, discounted cash flow techniques must be used to reflect the time value of money.